The Kitchen Cabinetmaker's Building and Business Manual

The Kitchen Cabinetmaker's Building and Business Manual

By Danny Proulx

Linden Publishing

FRESNO, CA

THE KITCHEN CABINETMAKER'S
BUILDING AND BUSINESS MANUAL

by

Danny Proulx

Disclaimer
Woodworking can be a dangerous profession. To prevent accidents, please be aware and work safely at all times. Power and hand tools are designed to cut wood and can easily injure the operators.
Some of the illustrations and photographs are shown without safety guards for reasons of clarity and are not meant to suggest that tools be used in this fashion. The authors, editors and publishers do not suggest that equipment be operated by poorly trained personnel. All the manufacturer's operating guidelines should be strictly followed to prevent accidents.
Due to varying conditions beyond our control, material quality, equipment safety features, and skill levels, neither the authors, editors, nor publishers assume any responsibility for accidents, injuries, damages or other losses.

© 1998 by Danny Proulx
All Rights Reserved

123456789

ISBN 0-941936-42-2

Library of Congress Cataloging-in-Publication Data

Proulx, Danny. 1947-
    The kitchen cabinetmaker's building and business manual /
written by Danny Proulx.
        p. cm.
    Includes index.
    ISBN 0-941936-42-2 (trade paper)
    1. Kitchen cabinets. 2. Cabinetwork--Handbooks, manuals, etc.
    3. Small business--Management--Handbooks, manuals, etc.
        I. Title.
TT197.5.K57P77   1998
643'.4--dc21   98-9883
                                    CIP

Printed in the United States of America
First Linden Publishing Edition 1998

LINDEN PUBLISHING

The Woodworker's
Library

Linden Publishing Company Inc.
336 West Bedford, Ste 107
Fresno, CA 93711 USA
800-345-4447
www.lindenpub.com

CONTENTS

INTRODUCTION

This business manual for the kitchen cabinetmaker is based on experience I have gained working for more than 20 years in the woodworking, home renovation and cabinetmaking trades. It is, in fact, a direct result of the many styles, tools and techniques I've worked with over those years.

This system, including the designs, construction practices, materials and supplies, as well as the cost- and retail price-calculations, reflects what I believe are the demands and needs of today's consumer. I have used this system exclusively in my company over the past five years and it has repeatedly proven its worth and flexibility.

Most of this manual will be devoted to business practices for the small kitchen cabinet company. A solid understanding of the principles required to successfully operate a small business is just as important as knowledge of cabinetmaking. The best kitchen cabinetmaker in the world will not be successful if the company is not run properly. There are far too many superb crafts people who are no longer in business because they ignored, or didn't take the time to study, good business practices.

The design of the kitchen cabinetmaking system featured in this book is not new or revolutionary, nor is it entirely my idea. It is a combination, based on my research, of the best qualities of European and North American kitchen cabinet construction styles. The final product, using these construction methods, results in a traditional North American face-frame style cabinet in any of the popular woods such as oak, cherry or maple, and also some of the newer cabinet materials in the industry such as plastic-coated medium-density fiberboard (MDF).

This design system produces a high-quality cabinet that equals or betters the products of middle- to high-end companies. The retail price of our finished product is higher than that of off-the-shelf lumber yard cabinets, but lower than prices charged by high-end companies. I know that my prices have proven to be competitive, because I have won my share of contracts from clients who have solicited multiple quotations.

Profit, based on the retail price structure that I will detail in this manual, can be calculated for each project. Cost analysis, also an important part of the project, will be covered in a separate chapter.

The bottom-line profit figure is based on many factors, not simply subtracting labor and material costs from the amount billed. It is a direct result of creating a good business plan and marketing strategy, and of having a sound knowledge of your customer's requirements. In short, the amount of net profit is directly related to your knowledge of operating a small business.

This best-of-blend cabinetmaking system is made possible by some recent innovations developed by the industry. The particle board screw now allows the cabinetmaker to produce extremely strong and stable butt joints with particle core boards. This cabinetry system also incorporates the high-quality European door hinge and adjustable cabinet legs with a traditional face frame cabinet. As well, it makes extensive use of the Euro bottom-mounted drawer slide system in standard cabinet drawers as well as in base and pantry pullouts. The result is a very high quality product.

There are few special tools required, beyond a good table saw and standard woodworking equipment. You don't need a largeworkforce. Many kitchen cabinetmakers operate out of converted garages or small industrial workshops.

Since I started using this design exclusively in my kitchen cabinetmaking business, I haven't encountered a situation to which I could not adapt this system Its proven excellence impresses me every time I complete a kitchen renovation project.

This manual will cover small business operations, cabinet design, manufacturing process, installation, special situations and cabinets, wholesale costs and cost analysis, profit analysis, and retail price schedules. I will also detail the materials needed and give you some supplier's names, although I believe the materials are readily available throughout the world. In short, you will have a complete kitchen cabinet business program. If you are already in the construction trades or if you are ready to start your own kitchen cabinetmaking business, either full- or part-time, this manual should answer most of your questions.

Dedication

Books are normally dedicated to a single person or persons who have been responsible in some way for the creation of the work. And, this book is no different—there are many people who have supported me and assisted me in the writing, photography, and illustrations included in this book. However, I'm dedicating this book to all the men and women who operate small businesses on a daily basis. They don't get enough credit for all the hours of hard work. It's a tough go, and often the lure of a regular nine to five job looks pretty inviting. But, they stick it out and all the applause should be theirs.

We're Open For Business

Joe's Kitchen Cabinetmaking Shop

Quality Custom Cabinets

CHAPTER 1

BUSINESS BASICS OVERVIEW

THE BUSINESS PLAN

"Why do we need a business plan? Let's just get the show on the road and open the doors. We've got a great idea, lots of talent, and a product that's sure to be a winner." If only it were that simple.

Business planning is a time-consuming and sometimes aggravating exercise, but it's also the most important task you'll ever undertake. Creating a thorough, well researched, and accurate document before opening the shop will lessen the chances of failure.

Past Opportunities

In earlier days, need generated the services provided. A blacksmith rode into town, realized that there wasn't a shop offering his services and, in no time, the new business was a success. Today, there are hundreds of people in our business fighting for the same market. Unlike the blacksmith, we have to sell our services to the consumer.

The Value of a Plan

What value is there in writing a business plan, and how can it help prevent failure? First, it allows you to analyze all the material that's been gathered and, before making any financial commitments, gives you an opportunity to look at the whole picture. If it becomes obvious, after gathering all this data, that the business isn't viable, you can get out before investing thousands of dollars.

Here is the first place where some new business people make a serious mistake. Belief in an idea is sometimes so strong that we often overlook, or choose not to believe, the negative aspects made obvious by well-documented research.

The completed business plan, at this point, becomes a fact-finding document. It should lead you to a question: Is the idea still valid after all the hard facts have been gathered? If you have doubts, get out at this point or approach the original idea from a safer angle. Second, it provides direction, like a road map to show you where the business is headed and to give you a course to follow. And third, it's a necessary document which provides information to the financial institutions that are going to invest in your company.

Creating the Plan

There are many sources available to business people who want information on writing a detailed plan. Libraries, the Internet, financial institutions, and many government departments can provide excellent outlines to follow, at little or no cost.

The business plan is divided into five major segments. These include information on the new company, market and industry information, marketing strategies, operational plans, and financial projections.

However, one important part of the plan is a summary of all the parts. Termed the executive summary, this one-page report is placed at the front of the plan. It highlights all the important data about the new business's management, services offered, target markets, promotion and financial matters. This page acts as a salesperson for the entire proposal and can play an important role in attracting interest. If well-written, this summary will help secure the proper financing. The goal is to secure adequate capital to support the business until it reaches the point where it will generate enough money to support itself.

Each of the sections following the executive summary page serves a specific purpose. The **company profile** details the form of business, such as sole proprietorship or partnership; its past history, proposed start date, location, classification and advisors (usually accountants and lawyers). **Market and industry analysis** should include information on industry trends, your product, the target market, research data, and a brief analysis of the competition. The **marketing strategy** lays out all the details of pricing strategy, how the product or services will be promoted, and the distribution plans. The **operating plan** describes the business's suppliers, manufacturing plans, operating regulations, and the human resources that are available.

The final section is devoted to the **financial plan** of the new business. This last area is often where many fail to address all the issues because they lack the expertise required. The result is a poor financial forecast, not based on reality, which may lead to disaster when an unexpected expense occurs.

Remember that bankers have little technical knowledge of our industry. Their skills are rooted in facts and figures. They will not look at the quality of your woodworking as much as at the accuracy of your financial forecasts. Their decision will be based on the cost of doing business and the sales projections. So be prepared, because they are trying to determine if these figures are realistic.

It's worth investing a couple of hours with an accountant to verify your data and, more importantly, to prepare you for the financial questions the bankers are sure to ask. Don't hesitate to spend extra money at this point for some valuable assistance.

To further lessen the chance of failure, I suggest you ask the accountants to review the entire plan as if they were potential investors. Would they be prepared to invest in the new business, based on the information provided?

I have often been annoyed by some of the questions and comments from accountants. However, they are looking at the situation from a dollars and cents point of view. It's a cold, hard, third-party review of the plan based on reality, and it can prevent mistakes by forcing you to take another look at your information.

Using the Plan

Once this plan is completed, it becomes your charter of operations. It is, in the most basic sense, a road map to show where the business is headed. And, keeping this map filed away in the glove compartment means the business will probably get off course.

All too often, the business plan is used strictly to arrange start-up capital from the bank. If this is successful, some people consider that the document has served its purpose. I know of small business owners who haven't referred to their original plan since opening the shop. It's no wonder they often experience difficulties.

One owner of a small woodshop had a plan created by business students at the local university. It proved to be an excellent decision because he got a well-researched and well-documented plan at a reasonable cost. The bank approved the business plan and loaned him the money he needed to open his shop. A year later, he was in trouble. Because I had been aware of the marketing recommendations in the original plan, I asked if the proposals in the plan had been unrealistic. He replied that he didn't know because he hadn't followed any of the suggestions. It was an unfortunate situation: He had been given all the information to show him how to market his new business, yet he chose to ignore the plan. Would it have made a difference if he had chosen to follow the business plan? I believe so, but after the first year, he was so deeply in debt that recovery was impossible.

The Bottom Line

One question should be asked during each monthly review. Did the business make a profit when comparing the cost of operations with the value of the sales generated? This review must be based on true costs, including your own labor rate.

The business-plan forecast includes sales and costs for three years into the future, usually a requirement with most lending institutions. Now, after two or three months in business, you have the advantage of projecting real data. Use the forecast percentage increases with the actual figures to estimate the year-end position. If there are potential problems, take corrective action now.

Existing Business Applications

Even if you have been in business for a year or two, don't discount the business plan. It can be used as a management tool to strengthen an existing business. Create the plan as if for a new venture, but study and use actual figures for the past years as your financial database. Project the sales increases based on population density, housing starts, or any other economic factors that may have an impact on your future operations. Once you've created a good baseline report for the current year, use the business plan for the monthly review process. There's an added bonus: This process forces you to create marketing strategies, which become your planning and budgetary guide for the new year. Because it's easier to predict the future if you know the past, existing businesses can benefit a great deal by investing a little time and money in the creation of a good business plan.

FINANCING

"What happened?" I asked when I saw a sign with the words *Gone Out Of Business* in big red letters. My woodworking friend replied, "They didn't have enough money to pay their bills. It's as simple as that." But, is it really that simple? The problem, obviously, was lack of funds, but the cause can be much deeper and is often the result of a combination of many poor decisions.

The financial road to success is tough and always uphill. Each day is filled with challenges and the need to choose which course to follow. Many decisions appear to be minor, and do not seem important enough to affect the overall wellbeing of the business. But, like trailers and trucks loaded with supplies, it's the total weight of all the small pieces that eventually damages the springs.

Bidding on Projects

Woodworkers often get themselves into trouble by not quoting properly for their work. I've seen some unbelievable examples of poor business sense in this area. Years ago, an associate told me that the profit margins were good on his projects. I was impressed and glad to hear he was doing well. I knew he had just completed a large job so I asked how he made out on that particular project. "Great," he said, "I made about 60% profit." Later in the conversation, I realized he was calculating his profit by subtracting the material costs from the amount billed. He hadn't accounted for all the other expenses such as shop overhead, operating costs and labor costs. Profit, calculated by his method, was good indeed.

Each job has associated costs. A portion of fixed and operating expenses, as well as the cost of labor, including your own time, must be included. Reviews should be completed quarterly, with an accountant if your skills are not adequate in this area, so that you can easily assign prorated amounts when calculating your quotes.

The accountant can provide fixed and operating working figures to use when determining project quotations. For example, based on its last yearly statement, a shop carries a weekly cost of $1,000 which includes rent, heat, light, power, telephone and taxes, called fixed costs. Operating costs, such as fuel, vehicle maintenance, repairs, etc., average about $500 per week. Labor, on a weekly basis, amounts to $1500. In this example, we know the shop carries a $3,000 weekly expense to operate. This figure is probably a little high for some shops but there are other costs such as equipment depreciation and administrative expenses, which I haven't specified, which are also included by an accountant.

A project billed at $7,000, with material costs at $3,300, would earn $3,700 gross profit. If this were the only project in the shop for the week, our net profit would be $700 dollars before our friends at the tax department take their share. That's a 10% net profit.

This example is rough, and the figures may be a little out of line for your shop, but it illustrates the need to apply real costs to every project. Assigned operating and fixed costs can be calculated and revised quarterly or half-yearly, depending on how often the expenses vary. Failure to be realistic when calculating project expenses means certain trouble.

Losing the Job

Often we bid low because we believe that our competition will get the work. Or as sometimes happens, the clients insinuate that they've received some very good prices and we overreact. Imagine bidding our sample job at $6,000 in order to be competitive. All the costs remain the same and we end up losing about $300.

In this type of situation it's better to let the low-ball competitors have the job, if such competitors really do exist. By accepting the work at a $300 loss you're not only losing money, you're also helping the competition because this can put your business in jeopardy. I realize that this is a difficult decision to make, but it's sometimes better to lose $300 instead of $3,000, which you would do if you had no other work. But, be aware of all of your operating costs so that you can at least break even when a situation like this occurs.

We'll always have those low-ballers who are willing to work for $5.00 an hour, but many successful shops combat this situation by selling quality instead of trying to meet every price. On one of my recent quotes, I was the highest bidder on a kitchen project and yet I won the job. After the clients signed the contract and told me the other quotes, I asked why they picked my company. "Simple," they said. "We liked your presentation album, the quality of your work, the fully detailed quote, and we followed your advice on comparing quality." So it really does work: You can bid properly, make a profit, and stay in business.

Spreading the Word

Advertising is a complicated subject. It's not unlike deciding which 20-story building to jump off. The end result is the same because your name will get out to the public, but you may get better exposure on the way down, depending on which building you choose.

How can you tell which advertising method is giving you the best return? I'll answer that question fully in another chapter. However, one gen-eral rule can be applied to prevent trouble: Try to set the advertising budget at the beginning of your business year, then stick to it.

The challenge will be in applying that budget fig-ure in the most effective ways, and that can be difficult. How do you know if the advertising dollars are working? Many successful business people simply ask clients how they learned about the company. In that way, they can track the amount spent on each advertising method against the return. Poorly managed ad programs have caused many businesses to fail.

Good Fiscal Management

Managing the financial portion of the business is just as important as producing quality work. One without the other will lead to certain failure. But how can we be both successful crafts people and good financial managers? Unfortunately, given today's economic situation, we have to find a way because we don't have a choice.

One way to avoid problems is to register with the adult education section of a local college offering night courses in small business manage-ment. Almost every successful business person I know has taken some form of business course. On closer examination, you'll discover that many talented woodworkers have lost their busi-nesses because they lacked financial management skills, or didn't pay enough attention to this crit-ical area.

Managing Material Costs

Materials are expensive. That is not news to any-one. Hardware, sheet goods, and finishing materials make up a sizable portion of the expenses with each project. Why, if this fact is so well known, do some shop owners not pay enough attention to managing the purchase and use of materials?

Depending on the type of work, material costs can be as much as 40% of the project. In our example, material amounted to $3,300. By exercising a little care and reducing waste, we may be able to reduce the expenditure by $100. That's a little more than 3% of the material cost. Those savings would add directly to the net bottom line. Over the period of a year, we could be realizing an additional $5,000 net profit simply by careful purchasing and managing material waste. We could probably cover two month's rent on a shop with that windfall.

I've visited many shops and seen open cans of contact cement drying up, sheet goods damaged by improper handling, hardware stored improperly, and general bad housekeeping practices. Just recently, I walked into a cabinet shop where the receiving door was wide open while everyone was at the coffee shop. I could have had a great time loading up my truck. And I'm sure they wouldn't have noticed anything missing, because of the extent of the mess. I won't be surprised to see that shop closed in the near future. The waste and mismanagement were deplorable.

Controlling material costs also means buying the product at the best available price. However, I don't suggest you buy poor quality hardware or tools. Over the long haul, that can cost more than any savings you've realized. Shop around

your area and check out the wholesale suppliers. Buy in quantity when possible, and ask the supplier for quantity purchase levels. Buying 100 loose-pack drawer slide sets, in place of 10 that are individually packaged, can reduce your costs substantially.

I'm hesitant to discuss the subject of employee theft because I've experienced it firsthand. I was very sad to discover that someone I trusted was stealing product from my business. Unfortunately, according to a police officer friend, theft by employees is more common than we'd care to believe. He suggested that business people be more aware of the possibility. He also said that the courts consider this breach of confidence to be more serious than common petty theft. It really makes me wonder what motivates people who abuse their position of trust. In some cases, theft can cause a business to fail and the employees to lose their jobs. It really is a no-win situation for everyone concerned.

Total Fiscal Management

Financial failure is often a slippery slope. Bad decisions compound until the shop is at the financial point of no return. Controlling expenditures by managing advertising, reducing waste, proper purchasing, and informed project quotations go a long way toward ensuring success. If you have these areas under control, your business will most likely be healthy.

LOCATION

Why is location so important? We should be able to open a shop anywhere, advertise, and wait for the clients to line up at our doors.

That's probably true to some extent, but is the money available to advertise and can we wait long enough until it all happens?

Location can play a decisive role in determining the success or failure of a new business. That role can be more or less serious depending on the types of products or services offered. Does the business depend upon pedestrian traffic flow, and is maximum exposure to the public a necessity? How much space is needed? And, is there a ready market in the area?

The Consumer Shop

If the business is consumer-oriented with products such as stock bookshelves, tables, and entertainment centers, visual exposure is necessary. Some woodworking shops, depending heavily on this type of traffic, have located in industrial parks and have soon discovered that they were losing the clients who buy on impulse. Many consumers, out for a Saturday afternoon of grocery shopping, haven't given a second thought to buying a coffee table. However, those products, displayed in a storefront window that shoppers are likely to pass, may trigger an interest.

The disadvantage is that shops located in a retail area with high traffic may have to limit production because of noise bylaws and the proximity of other stores. The sounds of our table saws and routers can put a strain on relationships with other store owners nearby.

One woodworking business, marketing goods built on speculation, located outside the city because of this factor. They produced hardwood tables, chairs, and other fine furniture as stock items and developed a beautiful line of high quality products. Business was good initially, due to the draw created by expensive high-profile advertising. However, they soon ran into trouble because the heavy cost of the advertising campaign, which was needed to draw the customers, put a serious strain on the business. They opened an additional retail outlet in a popular shopping center and the business is doing well once again because of the increased public exposure.

Targeted-market Shops

Woodworking shops that deal in commercial case goods and kitchen cabinets are not as dependent on location. Traffic flow and visual exposure can be an added bonus, but the rental rates common to high visibility locations, as well as some of the operating restrictions, do not always justify the cost.

Consumer awareness of this type of custom cabinet shop depends on word of mouth, targeted advertising, and some form of direct mail campaign. Money saved by locating in an industrial area can be used to fund advertising more effectively.

Market Area

Locating a shop far from the desired market can be disastrous in another sense. One kitchen cabinetmaking shop only considered rental rates, without giving any thought to the location of the primary market. The owners rented a shop in a new industrial park that was offering low rates to attract businesses, but the majority of the homes in the area were recently built. Those homeowners wouldn't need kitchen cabinets for years, so the cabinetmaker was forced to travel long distances to each job site. The cost of labor and travel added greatly to his project expenses.

Local recognition is an important factor with any proposed location. For example, it's not uncommon to see two or three good woodworking shops in a rural area. It seems to be a desirable location in our trade. But, if you do decide to set up shop near other cabinetmakers, make sure your market studies include an analysis of population density in relation to the number of shops already in existence.

New shops often take a while to get established in rural communities because they're considered outsiders. Failure is not uncommon in this situation, so be prepared for the long haul. Rural business owners are often involved in minor league sports organizations, service clubs and other neighborhood activities, which help them make the transition from outsider to local more easily.

The Home Shop

Over the last few years there seems to be a trend towards locating the shop and the home together. This is particularly true with one- or two-person shops. Of course, local zoning regulations must permit this type of operation. Don't even consider a home shop situation until you've checked with local officials. You can be forced to close down if you don't follow zoning rules.

The home shop has many advantages but it requires self-discipline on the part of the woodworker. It's possible to get involved in home and family activities instead of paying attention to the problems of running a woodworking shop. In my case, I've located a shop behind the house and, for the most part, haven't regretted the decision. However, there are times when shop work, like organizing inventory and cleaning, take a back seat to other more interesting events around the home. If my business were located in an industrial park, possibly I wouldn't have any such distractions, and the shop cleaning would be done immediately. So, be aware of both the positive and the negative factors before making a decision.

Location Awareness

I've never met a business owner to whom rental cost wasn't a concern. Rent can be a huge financial drain on a company, so it has to provide a good return on the investment. The goal is to get the best location for the money available.

Be aware of the other businesses in the area. The decision on location should be based on the quality of services in that area. Ask yourself questions such as: Are there popular businesses close by that will draw potential clients to the shop?

The area should also have easy access. I know of one high-profile grocery store that opened a second location on a busy street, yet it closed in less than six months. The management hadn't considered that this street, with thousands of cars passing daily, was also divided by a median. Many motorists wouldn't bother to negotiate a U-turn at the next intersection just to get back to the store. The store was also located on the side with morning rush hour traffic. On the commuter's return drive, they found the median between them and the store. The store owners attempted to have the city install a break in the median with a turning lane, but were unsuccessful. However, if they had located on the other side of the road, with easy access for the shoppers going home after work, it might have been a successful business. I was one of many people who hadn't seen the potential for failure. Decisions that determine success or failure can be that simple.

Renting or Buying

A businessman once told me that he only bought companies in order to acquire property. He reasoned that most businesses have difficulty getting paid for goodwill when the operation is sold. His business, he said, would be sold to fund his retirement. Therefore, he planned to make a reasonable living while operating the shop, and the company would purchase the building. When he was ready to retire, he would be able to sell both the business and the property.

Buying or renting the property is a choice worth considering. The money has to be paid out one way or another, so it might be worthwhile to look at the potential value of purchasing a building. An accountant can analyze all the related issues of interest rates, taxes, and operating expenditures for you and help with your decision.

Location Analysis

The choice of location can have an impact on the success of the business. During the research stage, when the business plan is being written, consider the following questions:

1. Is the area easily accessible and reasonably well known?

2. Are there other businesses in the area that will provide a draw to potential clients of your business?
3. Are the surrounding streets and buildings clean and well kept, making the area an inviting place?
4. Is the location close to the target market?
5. What is the potential for target market growth near the business?
6. Can the shop be expanded in the future?
7. If this is a rental property, are the owners concerned about building maintenance?
8. How much space is available?
9. Is public transportation available for staff and clients?

There are many more questions, depending on the proposed shop's style of operation. But simply stated, location is a primary consideration and, in some cases, can have a tremendous impact on the health of your new business. As the grocery store owner discovered, ignoring small details can mean failure.

SETTING UP SHOP

Will your woodworking shop be used to display sample products? Do you plan to have clients visit your business? If you've answered yes to these questions, it's time to take a critical look at shop set-up.

A clean, well organized woodworking shop, with a comfortable area for your customers, makes a positive subconscious statement about you and about your work. Have you ever hired a contractor who arrived at the job site driving a muddy, beat-up old truck? You watch him as he gathers tools that are scattered about in the back of the truck, loads them into an old milk crate, and heads in to work. What were your first thoughts? Not very impressive, right?

Imagine yourself as a customer entering your shop. First impressions, whether conscious or subconscious, can have a profound effect on a client. Would you sign a contract for a $10,000 kitchen with someone who couldn't find a pen under the mounds of paper work on the desk, let alone the table saw which you think you can discern under a pile of sawdust? You'd probably be looking for some excuse to leave as quickly as possible.

Presentation

A friend of mine, who is a chef , tells me that presentation is the most important part of any meal she serves. "If the food looks good," she says, "the customers believe it will taste good." That may not always be the case, but at least everyone is starting on a positive note.

Woodworking shops are noisy, dusty places. That's the nature of our work, but clients come to our shops with a mental impression of the finished product: a beautiful entertainment center, a dining room table, or a clean modern kitchen with all the latest features. That image can be shattered if they walk into a woodworking war zone.

Look around the area where you live. Investigate some of the businesses that have closed. Often, there appears to be a lack of organization, with customer-service areas that look like they're one step above the city dump. Would you do business with a shop like that? I'd have second thoughts about bringing my dog there, let alone writing

them a check for their services. Presenting your shop and your product in a professional manner is extremely important. It can be, and has been, the difference between success and failure in many cases.

Shop Layout

During the initial stages of new-business planning, visit various service shops in the area. Look at the businesses that seem to be inviting. How do they present their goods or services? Is the area well lit, giving an impression that they're not trying to hide anything? Is the shop clean, comfortable and well organized?

A good example is an automobile dealership. We all know that a garage is an uninviting space, with grease, oil, and broken car parts. But, take a look at the reception center: clean, bright, with music in the background, service managers wearing sparkling white coats, and free coffee for the clients. Car dealers know the value of comfortable surroundings.

When planning a woodworking shop, two different spaces must be considered: First, the production area, and second the showroom or customer-service area. Many clients don't know, or care very little, about a beautiful table saw. They want to see examples of your cabinet work in pleasant surroundings.

Dividing these two areas properly is vital. If possible, plans should account for the noise and dust factors between the two spaces. Walls that are well sealed, and lined with noise-reducing insulation, are often a requirement. The client area doesn't necessarily have to be large, but it should be quiet, clean and bright. If possible, the display should reflect a natural setting for the product.

Production Planning

It's difficult to detail specific layout procedures for woodworking shops because of the varied products we produce. There isn't any one design that will ensure success. The goal is to maximize the production of goods from raw materials to the finished stage. This is commonly called workflow.

The time required to build a quality cabinet is determined by its design and by our ability. However, wasting time trying to find tools and shop supplies adds unnecessarily to that time, and results in a reduced profit. If you want to market your products at a competitive price, you must have an efficient shop.

Administrative Planning

We wear many hats in our business. For the small shop, that often means being the president of the company and also performing all the tasks of a janitor. Included in those duties are the administrative functions of recordkeeping, invoicing, creating construction drawings, and bookkeeping, to name a few. Most of these duties are time-consuming, however, they are also necessary to the wellbeing of the business. As we all know, most of these hours cannot be charged to our customers.

How, then, do we reduce the time required to complete administrative duties? Hiring someone to perform these functions is an obvious and simple solution but that may not be possible for many small shops. Another option is to use tech-

nology, particularly a computer with software programs designed for small- and medium-sized businesses.

Computers in the Woodworking Shop

Drive by many small businesses in the evening and you'll often see the lights on well past midnight. Often, some poor soul is struggling with the mounds of paperwork necessary in today's modern shop. Monthly summaries for taxes collected, employee deductions, as well as invoicing and accounts receivable, must be completed if we want to stay in business. Shops that ignore or delay reporting usually end up with more trouble than they can handle. Banks and government departments do not have unlimited patience with businesses that fail to comply with the regulations. Some might say that they don't have a sense of humor, but of course I would never say such a thing. My old woodworking partner often said, "If they can't take a joke, to hell with them." But, in reality, it's a serious matter.

Shop set-up plans, for the new or existing business, should include the use of computers. Software designed to produce drawings for the shop quickly, as well as software for managing the administrative support services, can greatly reduce non-productive hours.

Computer-aided Drawing

Most kitchen cabinetmaking shops now use, or would benefit by using, computer-aided drawing (CAD) programs to produce floor plans and elevation drawings for the client. Incorporated in many of these programs is the ability to calculate retail quotations, job costs, sheet cutting dimensions, and materials lists. Costing between $2,000 and $10,000, these programs can be quite an expenditure for many shops but the payback time, in terms of hours saved versus manual drawings and proposals, is normally short.

There is also another benefit gained by the use of CAD programs which relates back to the section on presentation. Most customers are impressed with the proposals generated by these software programs. The three-dimensional feature included in many CAD programs is an excellent and effective sales tool.

Administrative Software

Accounting software programs are numerous, so it's difficult to recommend one that will suit your business. However, good fully-featured packages cost between $100 and $300. Most will perform basic bookkeeping functions such as tracking expenditures and accounts receivable, recording taxes collected and generating invoices.

Talk to other business owners about accounting software to determine which programs best suit your needs. Some software companies have a trial version available and many software dealers have demonstration programs at their stores. In my opinion, accounting software is an invaluable tool. It has reduced our shop's administrative tasks to hours instead of days.

Shop Set-up for the Future

The shop set-up plan is just as important as the business plan. It takes into consideration all the issues developed in the business plan and implements the procedures in a practical sense. We're going to sell this, manufacture that, and operate the shop so that we maximize profits. The shop set-up plan should lay it out, step by step. You don't want to say, "Oops, I never thought of that."

Consider all the functions necessary in producing your product. Detail the movements on a diagram before setting up any equipment. Follow the raw materials through the shop, including the procedures required at each piece of equipment. Does it make sense? Are you moving material unnecessarily in the workshop, wasting time and effort? Remember, lost time and wasted materials reduce the net profit.

Equally important are the administrative processes associated with the business. These non-productive functions must be reduced. By using computer technology, we improve efficiency and, in most cases, have a more up-to-date picture of the business's finances.

Why do some companies fail? Often it's a simple matter of not putting into practice all the well-designed theory in the business plan. If it looks good on paper, and it can be practically applied in real terms, the business should produce the desired results.

ADVERTISING AND MARKETING

Does advertising really work, and is it worth the money it costs? Well, in the most basic sense, if we don't put up a sign, or fail to tell anyone we're in business, we won't have any work. We all know that bit of news. But where do we begin, how much money is needed, and what are the most effective advertising methods?

We already discussed advertising briefly, but in this section I want to dig deeper into this complex subject. First, it is worthwhile to define the major forms of advertising available to the woodworking shop and to look at some of the pitfalls.

Advertising promotions can be classified as targeted or direct, general and soft. These are broad definitions, but most of the advertising for a cabinet shop can be categorized under those headings. That's the where and what part of the equation, now we have to decide how much money is needed.

Targeted Advertising

Reaching only those people who are most likely to use your service is called direct or targeted marketing. For example, a restoration contractor would normally send his brochures to areas of the city that contain mostly older homes. Campaigning in a new subdivision, for this type of service, would not be effective.

How do you know who to target? That's a key question and it is not easily answered. First, it's necessary to define who the most likely end user would be for your services. One successful campaign was started by a local business specializing in period furniture, specifically country style tables, chairs, and deacon's benches. The management reasoned that those most interested would be readers of a magazine that catered to the country lifestyle. A mailing list was purchased from this magazine and a brochure was sent to readers who

lived within a 50-mile radius of the woodworking shop. It turned out to be a successful promotion.

There are, however, many failed campaigns for each one that is successful. Direct mail can be expensive given the cost of printing, envelopes, and postage, often in the range of 40 to 50 cents a letter. To increase your odds of success, research the intended market.

General Advertising

This type of advertising is not geared to any specific target group, but is concerned mainly with raising the recognition-value of the business. Commonly, ads would be placed in newspapers and magazines describing the businesses location and its product line. Potential clients would see something like *Joe's Cabinet Shop, Fine Quality Cabinets at Reasonable Prices* with an address and telephone number. Hopefully, someone will read the ad who needs such services or who will remember the name when a need arises.

This form of advertising is a necessary part of business. The trade name must be recognized in order to establish a comfort level for those purchasing your services. Ideally, when customers are shopping around and come across the name, they'll think, "Yes, I've heard of that business."

If you have unlimited funds, mass media campaigns will raise the business profile quickly. However, managing a realistic advertising budget skillfully means finding media publications that will maximize exposure at a reasonable cost. That old saying, "Getting the best bang for your buck," is appropriate in this case.

Advertising always seems to me to be a race against the clock. The returns, in the form of workload increases, must be constantly monitored. One question is common to all businesses. How much money can we afford to spend and will the workload increase, in a reasonable time period, enough to justify the expenditure? Unfortunately, without expenditure control and planning, some businesses lose the race.

Soft Advertising

Sponsoring a minor league baseball team, participating in community activities, or supporting local events are forms of soft advertising. These are not the in-your-face kind of promotion. However, soft advertising can be effective in creating a community-minded image for the business. It's considered giving something back to the community that has patronized your operation. But the expenses must be closely monitored, as you will receive many requests for your support and must choose between many local teams and events.

Choosing the Medium

Do we take the shotgun approach and try to reach everyone, or do we target the most likely users? That's an important question and, when answered incorrectly, can mean financial hardship. But, there are ways to help determine which method is best for your business.

After the budget has been set, decide which product or service you want to feature. If your business is offering a wide range of goods and services, choose one that will appeal to a large group of clients. Make the ad as simple and direct as

possible so that the reader isn't required to absorb a lot of material. Expand the range of interest for that product, if possible. For example, in my business, I often advertise cabinets for the kitchen, the laundry room, the storage area, and the workshop. They are basically the same type of cabinet, but I may interest someone who wouldn't normally consider having laundry room cabinets made by a kitchen cabinetmaker.

If the business is new and a well-defined potential market can be identified, direct mail advertising can create a demand quickly. If the shop is located in a small town or village, large display ads in local papers will often generate work. Ads in these village or local area newspapers are reasonably priced and the results can be easily monitored.

Budget Considerations

In times such as these, expenditures must be closely monitored. Advertising, being one of the major expenses, requires a lot of attention if we are to realize maximum return. One of the best methods to ensure a measure of control is to set your advertising budget at the beginning of the year and stick to it.

Problems occur when spending gets out of control. For those of us currently in business, it's normal to receive two or three calls a week from people who want our advertising dollars. While the majority of these proposals can be effective, we must stick by our budgetary plan.

I've known businesses who have experienced serious financial difficulty because they've bought into every new advertising proposal that came their way. By doing so, they made two basic errors in small business management: First, not setting a budget and, second, investing in an advertising program without taking a hard look at the effectiveness of the promotional medium.

Determining the Budget

Calculating the yearly advertising budget is determined by analyzing all the facts and figures that are used to create the business plan. This calculation applies to new businesses creating a first-time plan or an existing business writing next year's operational plan.

In the section on financing, we covered assigning expenditures to determine the shop's monthly operational costs. Advertising is part of those costs, and it's necessary to be as accurate as possible when determining these costs, so enlisting the help of an accountant can be a wise investment.

Now, after all the calculations have been analyzed, you've set an advertising budget of $5000 per year. It's critical, for the financial wellbeing of the business, that you stay within this amount. The creative challenge will be to use that money in the most effective method possible. As we all know, it's not an easy task. There are many tempting advertising promotions that arise during the year.

Take the case of a businessman who had a passion for gadgets. Many of us do, and I'll be the first to admit guilt on that count, but his love for these promotional toys had a serious negative effect on the business. I'd walk into his office and see boxes of pens with the company name, refrigerator

magnets, T-shirts, ball caps, note pads and many other promotional items. His collection grew to the point of being ridiculous. Sadly, the following year, I saw all those items in a business liquidator's showroom. Those small, seemingly inexpensive advertising items ended up being very expensive indeed for this man.

Analyzing Expenditures

Controlling the advertising budget and the number of dollars spent each year is an important exercise. However, directing those dollars to the most effective areas, so that maximum exposure is realized, can be just as important as the amount of money spent. If you're not getting results, your money is wasted.

ESTABLISHING A WORKFORCE

In the initial planning stages for a kitchen cabinetmaking shop, you must decide on the method of operation. Will you have full-time staff members, part-time staff, or occasional employees to help with the more awkward tasks?

Many kitchen cabinetmakers operate their business as a one-person shop and, most of the time, it's possible to manage that way. However, there are times when two or more people are required. Cutting four by eight sheets of board, transporting cabinets to the job site and installing cabinets are jobs that often require two people. Then, employing someone on a temporary basis is a good idea, providing you have a couple of part-timers who can help on short notice. This is how I operate my business. I employ four people who are available when I need them. My workforce is made up of a retired person, two shift workers and, most importantly, my wife. All are more than happy to make a few extra dollars while learning about kitchen cabinetmaking. I do, however, need to know my staff's schedules, so that I can plan shop and installation tasks for times when someone is available. And, for the most part, there is little inconvenience.

Another way to handle your staffing needs is to employ regular part-time staff. You may want to hire someone for 10 to 20 hours per week until your business reaches a level of volume requiring full-time employees.

Part-time staffing can be a problem if you don't have access to a large workforce. Try inquiring at local trade schools and colleges: Many students do not have a full calendar of classes and most can work as much as three to four hours each day. Additionally, there are many part-timers who work for other businesses who would be happy to work for you on the same basis. Again, scheduling your workflow to accommodate these people is often easily accomplished.

If your volume gets to the point where a full-time staff is required, certain procedures, labor practice regulations, and accounting functions must be addressed. But, for the most part, the added paper work associated with a good full-time employee is a minor consideration in a successful business. We'll go over some of the questions involving full-time staff in a later chapter.

BUILDING THE CABINETS

Building kitchen cabinets isn't a difficult process.

Anyone with a basic knowledge of common woodworking practices can easily complete all the required tasks. Once the design is decided upon, assembly is straightforward. However, the design phase can sometimes be the most challenging operation.

Kitchen Design

Study the chapter on kitchen design in this manual. Look at kitchens in the homes of your friends and relatives. Try to analyze the good and bad points of each layout. Ask questions of the person who uses that space daily. You'll soon begin to see what is bad or good and what changes have to be made to the existing kitchens you're about to renovate.

Cabinetry Design

As briefly mentioned, the design featured in this manual is a hybrid cabinet. It uses all the positive design aspects developed by the Europeans to create the traditional-looking North American style cabinet.

This North American hybrid incorporates the Euro carcass (box) style, hinges, drawer glides and adjustable base cabinet legs in a wooden face-framed cabinet with a solid raised-panel or plywood panel door.

This design allows us to build a freestanding, modular cabinet that is stronger and higher in quality than most cabinets on the market today. The retail price falls in the middle range between the inexpensive factory-made boxes and high-end custom cabinets. However, its quality is comparable to the best units on the market.

Face Frame or Frameless

The hybrid cabinet dimensions can be easily modified to build a European frameless cabinet when the need arises. If the client wants a white Euro style cabinet, we simply eliminate the wood face frame and install particle core board (PCB) doors with high pressure laminate surfaces. We'll detail the design later in this manual.

MAINTAINING THE MOMENTUM

Once your business is up and running, you need to continue doing all the positive things that got you to this point. It's an ongoing and sometimes exhausting process, but you must maintain the momentum if you want to succeed.

Analyzing the Results

Everything that causes a reaction or an impact on your business must be analyzed. What did you do right or wrong? Did an advertising promotion result in remarkable returns? If it did, ask yourself why. What was so unique that made people respond so well?

It's just as important to analyze failed advertising campaigns. If a program failed miserably, investigate the reasons. There is value in learning from mistakes so that they can be avoided in the future.

The Planning Process

We'll look at some areas that need to be considered as ongoing processes: How to maintain the level of interest in the business and how to use a client base to gain free advertising. A satisfied client is one of the most valuable resources for a business. We'll discuss how that resource is best managed.

In the final analysis, it's not just how good we are as cabinetmakers, it's how good we are in the business of cabinetmaking. The best craftsperson in the world won't be self-employed long if he can't operate a business and, conversely, the best businessperson won't survive when selling an inferior product. It's a subtle marriage and, to be successful, we have to combine two different disciplines.

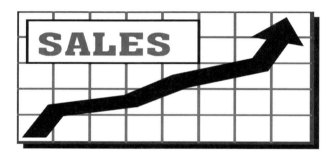

CHAPTER 2

THE BUSINESS PLAN

Why do small businesses fail? There are many factors and, sadly, in a survey made by the federal government, we see that 80% of small businesses fail in the first five years. The reasons are varied but the most common are well known.

Failure is most often due to inadequate planning before the business is open. The business plan wasn't prepared, nor was a feasibility study done. Cash flow projections were not created.

We'll concentrate on the business plan in this chapter. However, other reasons for failure will also be covered. These include inadequate funding to start the business, as well as insufficient ongoing sources of money to support the operation. Lack of training and experience in management also ranks in the top five causes for failure.

Picking the wrong location, poor inventory management, failure to account for the cost of equipment needed, and improper control of client credit limits, also add to the list of problems that had been experienced by failed businesses.

Some of the other causes include expanding too quickly, less than acceptable recordkeeping practices, and an attitude that prevents the business

person from seeking the help of professionals such as bankers, lawyers, and accountants.

All these matters should be, and must be, addressed in the business plan. We're crafts people but, if we decide to sell our goods and services, we have to be equally competent business managers in order to succeed.

DETERMINING BUSINESS STYLE

If you don't know where you want to go, you obviously don't need a plan on how to get there. It's as simple as that. However, if you have a goal, even something simple like wanting to be rich and successful, planning goes a long way to ensuring that you'll reach your target.

Opening a business is the goal of many people. But what type of business? Before any other plans are made, you should try to determine your abilities. Do you have any experience in the area of the proposed new business? Have you worked in the field, either part-time or for someone else? Many of us who eventually start our own businesses have worked in the trade for a number of years and have developed technical and business expertise. Experience lessens the risks involved when opening your own shop.

Before planning the actual method of operation, gather as much information as possible on the proposed business, specifically information on the competition and the consumer needs. If the market is saturated with cabinet shops in your area and the consumer's demands are being met, it may be wise to look elsewhere. If your idea is new and revolutionary, will it fill a need? And will there be a demand for your services?

FACTS AND FIGURES

There are certain matters you should address prior to creating a business plan. The following is a list of questions that you should answer. It will be beneficial to write out the answers in a detailed form so you can review them periodically.

1. Provide a description of the new business.
2. What is your preferred location and why?
3. Explain the product or services being offered.
4. What experience do you have in the cabinet making field?
5. Will the business be a sole proprietorship, partnership, etc., and what is the new name for the company?
6. Describe the equipment and supplies required, with current costs.
7. Who will handle the daily bookkeeping, invoicing and ordering?
8. How do you plan to finance the first year of operation?
9. Detail the questions involving worker's insurance, liability insurance, and local business licenses.
10. What financial and material resources will you bring into the new business?
11. Outline the payroll requirements (including yourself and the part-time help) for the first year.

There may also be other factors to consider in this initial look at the new business. Some will be appropriate and unique to your business, so list

and explain these in detail. The written pre-business investigation, if well-documented, can be used as a letter of introduction to bankers, lawyers, accountants and potential investors.

It's often easier to send this document to these people before meeting with them so they will have an understanding of the new operation. It saves time and money, explains everything in detail, and is a professional approach to dealing with the financial and legal community.

> **Tip: NAME THE PLAN**
> *Call this document the Proposed Business Overview. The name conveys the message that you are still investigating all possibilities and are open to suggestion and/or advice.*

LEGAL HELP

There are many jokes about lawyers, and I'm sure lawyers are tired of hearing all the negative comments people make about them. However, a knowledgeable legal advisor can save a business person a great deal of time and prevent a great deal of frustration.

There are many bylaws, regulations, legal documents, worker's compensation rules, and questions of liability and responsibilities. Studying these can take valuable time that should be spent doing business. Every hour dealing with paper work is an hour of income lost. A craftsperson can become swamped by all these details.

How, then, can we pay attention to all these rules and regulations efficiently? Many business people have a lawyer review such documents and explain them in plain, simple language. Ask the lawyer: What are my responsibilities, my liabilities, and how do I meet the necessary requirements? Once the answers are understood, make a decision, then get on with the job of cabinetmaking. It's an easy and effective way to deal with the requirements and, in the long run, is usually less expensive.

However, you wouldn't hire a plumber to install a light fixture, so don't hire a lawyer who doesn't specialize in small business. Ask if the law practice caters to small business and inquire about similar businesses they represent. There is a different set of legal skills required in criminal law and in business law.

ACCOUNTANTS

Using the services of an accountant is not necessary when starting a new business. But, like a good lawyer, a good accountant can be an inexpensive form of insurance. The financial community looks favorably on a proposed business venture that uses an accountant to prepare loan applications.

In certain states and provinces an accountant is required to provide a certified business audit for a limited or incorporated company. Often, banks demand that accountants be used to certify the financial statement of the principals who are opening a new business.

Accountants are a good sounding board to use when reviewing your new business plan. They will make suggestions, analyze the facts and figures, and prepare you for the questions that

bankers are sure to ask. An experienced small-business accounting firm deals with hundreds of similar-sized operations and has access to all the current financial data. More often than not, your accountant will be familiar with lending institutions that are offering the best rates. They will also know if your new business qualifies for any low-cost government loan programs.

It can seem expensive to use an accounting firm until you realize that they may be able to reduce the rate of interest on a loan. Two or three percentage points off a $50,000 loan, over a five-year term, amounts to a great deal of money. If you subtract the cost of an accountant from the amount saved, you may well come out on the plus side.

> **Tip: CALL FOR CONSULTATION**
> *When searching for lawyers and accountants to represent your business interests, call and ask for an initial consultation. Many professionals offer a free first-time meeting to discuss their services.*

PREPARING THE PLAN

First, a well-written plan helps convince potential financial partners to invest capital. The plan is the sales pitch for financing.

Second, the plan is a critical management tool. It provides a realistic look at the activities of the new venture. The business plan is a feasibility study. Evaluation through market research, operational planning, and financial projections determine whether or not the proposed business will be viable. It's your future that's on the line and you will want to know as much as possible before you start. After you complete the research, it may be obvious to you that there is simply too much at risk.

The Outline

This business plan is based on an outline published by the U.S. Small Business Administration. There are many plan forms available to the new business owner. They have been well researched and you'll find it's worth the time and effort it takes to complete them accurately and with as much detail as possible.

1. Executive Summary
2. The Business
    A. Description of business
    B. Marketing
    C. Competition
    D. Operating procedures
    E. Personnel
3. Financial Data
    A. Loan applications
    B. Capital equipment and supply list
    C. Balance sheet
    D. Break-even analysis
    E. Profit & Loss Statements
       - Three-year summary
       - Detail by month, first year
       - Detail by quarters, second and third years
       - Assumptions upon which projections were based
4. Cash Flow Projections
    - Follow guidelines in number 3
5. Supporting Documents
    - Tax returns of principals for last three years

- Personal financial statement
- Copy of proposed lease or purchase agreement for building space
- Copy of licenses and other legal documents
- Copy of resumes of all principals
- Copies of letters of intent from suppliers, etc.

The Executive Summary

At one time, I thought an executive summary was nonsense. I felt that any executive who didn't have time to read my complete plan wasn't worth meeting. Since then, I've learned that this section is the bait. If it is well-written, an investor or a banker will take the hook and read the proposal. Many plans have failed at this point because the investor's interest wasn't piqued or the banker wasn't impressed.

Remember, most products are sold on the strength of the packaging. This summary should give the reader an overview. In effect, it is the package for the business plan. It should introduce the managers and owners as well as the product or service. It should refer to plans for the promotion and marketing of the product or service. A summary of projections, loan requirements and a repayment schedule should also be provided. Keep the summary short. One page is ideal. Most importantly, put it at the front of the plan, but prepare it last, so that all important points are included.

Description of Business

In this section, provide a detailed description of your business. An excellent question to ask yourself is: "What business am I in?" In answering this question, include your products, market and services as well as a thorough description of what makes your business unique. Remember that as you develop your business plan, you may have to modify or revise your initial questions.

The business description section is divided into three primary sections. The first section describes your business; the second section, the product or service you will be offering, and the third section details the location of your business, explaining why this location is desirable.

Section 1 - Describing Your Business

When describing your business, you should explain:

1. Legalities - business form: proprietorship, partnership, corporation, franchise.
2. What licenses or permits you will need.
3. Business type: merchandising, manufacturing or service.
4. What your product or service is.
5. Is it a new independent business, a takeover, an expansion, a franchise?
6. Why your business will be profitable.
7. What are the growth opportunities?
8. How will franchising impact on growth opportunities?
9. When your business will be open (days, hours).
10. What you have learned about your kind of business.

Section 2 - Your Product/ Service Description

In this section describing your business, try to outline the benefits of your goods and services from your customers' perspective. Successful business owners know or at least have an idea what their customers want or expect from them. This anticipation can be helpful in building customer satisfaction and loyalty. It certainly is a good strategy for beating the competition and retaining your competitive edge.

Describe what you are selling, how your product or service will benefit the customer, which products or services are in demand and what is different about the product or service you're offering.

Section 3 - Detailing The Location

The description of business section should also include the location of your business and how you believe it can play a decisive role in your success. Your location should be built around your customers, it should be accessible, and it should provide a sense of security.

Detail the answers to these questions when addressing this section of your business plan: What are your location needs? What kind of space will you need? Why is the area or building desirable? Is it easily accessible? Is public transportation available? And, is street lighting adequate?

Marketing

Marketing plays a vital role in successful business ventures. How well you market your product or service, along with a few other considerations, will ultimately determine your degree of success or failure. The key element of a successful marketing plan is to know your customers, their likes, their dislikes and their expectations. By identifying these factors, you can develop a marketing strategy that will allow you to arouse their interest and fulfill their needs.

Identify your customers by their age, sex, income level, education level and type of residence. At first, target only those customers who are most likely to purchase your product or service. As your customer base expands, you may need to consider modifying the marketing plan to include other customers.

Develop a marketing plan for your business by answering these questions.

1. Who are your customers? Define your target market(s).
2. Are your markets growing? steady? declining?
3. Is your market share growing? steady? declining?
4. Are your markets large enough to expand?
5. How will you attract, hold, increase your market share?

Pricing and Sales

The retail price of goods and services is an integral part of the market plan. Your pricing strategy is another marketing technique you can use to improve your overall competitiveness. Although your competitive edge will be based on your own prices, it is a good idea to get a feel for the pricing strategy your competitors are using. That way, you can determine if your prices are in line with competitors in the area.

The key to a successful pricing strategy is to have a well-defined plan. It's important to constantly monitor your competitor's offerings and the quality of goods or services offered by your competition. If your prices are higher, because the quality you offer is superior, detail the reasons in the business plan.

The pricing strategy is also controlled, to some extent, by the cost of your goods and services. Detailed explanations as well as your control or monitoring procedures should be explained.

Advertising

An explanation of advertising methods and long-range advertising plans are an integral part of marketing a small business. How are you going to advertise on a monthly basis? What types of advertising do you plan on doing? Describe the preferred types of advertising and the reasons for their use. Detail the percentage of your advertising budget that will be allocated to general, direct and soft advertising programs. Illustrate how these different campaigns will be measured and monitored.

Competition

Competition is a way of life. We compete for scholarships, jobs and promotions. We compete in sports and in almost every aspect of our lives. Nations compete for the consumer in the global marketplace as do individual business owners. Advances in technology can send the profit margins of a successful business into a tailspin, causing them to plummet overnight or within a few hours. When considering these and other factors, we can conclude that business is a highly competitive, volatile arena. Because of this, it is important to know your competitors.

Analyze your competition by asking the following questions.

1. Who are your five nearest direct competitors?
2. Who are your indirect competitors?
3. How are their businesses: steady? increasing? decreasing?
4. What have you learned from their operations? from their advertising?
5. What are their strengths and weaknesses?
6. How does their product or service differ from yours?

Operating Procedures

The operational procedure gives the investors an overview of how the business will function. It should deal with general management and financial issues. Areas that should be addressed are:

1. How important are suppliers to the business?
2. Location details.
3. Terms and conditions of business purchase, if applicable.
4. The main contact person.
5. Trade volume discounts.
6. Minimum order requirements from suppliers.
7. Any trade restrictions.
8. Product availability.
9. Shipping procedures.
10. Exclusive rights to resell or use a product.

Personnel

Provide a detailed description of all personnel involved in the business. Explain every person's place in the company, their duties and their activity levels in the day-to-day operation. Include yourself in the description.

Silent partners and professional personnel, such as the company lawyer and accountant, are also important. Lending institutions consider these non-salaried personnel as support staff and they are an important asset.

Financial Data

This section of the business plan outline is self-explanatory. However, don't make the mistake of not including enough data. As the old carpenter once said, "Better one nail too many than one too few."

It may be necessary to have an accountant assemble all the data into a format that will make sense to prospective lenders. I often find financial projections and statements to be outside my field of expertise, but I want to present an informative, accurate package, so I often hire an accountant to handle these tasks.

This would be an ideal time for you to review and try to understand the financial projections. You will be faced with questions, so if you can't afford to have an accountant with you when you meet the investors, be prepared with the answers.

Supporting Documents

These records are provided to the lenders to support all the claims and projections in the plan. Information should be provided listing the sources of your statistics. If you've based your sales on population density, provide census information from local or federal government departments.

If sales projections were based on the fact that housing starts were on the increase in your business area, support those claims with documents. Sales increases are normally based on population growth, home building trends, the number of rental properties compared with the number of owner-occupied residences, new industry starts, and other trend data that is often free and readily provided by local governments. Don't hesitate to include these documents as they add to the business plan's credibility.

The Completed Document

When you are finished writing the plan, review it with knowledgeable business people you trust. It's important that you fully understand all the information supplied in this document. You will be questioned on a number of points by the financial institutions.

Remember, this plan is your road map.

> **Tip: MAKE COPIES**
> *Prepare multiple copies of your business plan. A few days prior to meeting with bankers, send them a copy of your plan so that they can familiarize themselves with your new company.*

CHAPTER 3

FINANCING

Will you need to borrow money to start your new business? That's an easy question to answer because most of us do need extra capital to get any operation off to a good start. The problem is determining how much you'll need, and what it will cost you to borrow it.

Many lenders expect business owners to provide some percentage of the total funds required. In some cases, depending on the risk, it could be as high as 50% of the amount needed. And, in many instances, banks want a personal guarantee for the loan, regardless of the company's legal status.

BANK FINANCING

All businesses, regardless of size, need working capital, or cash flow, to support their growth. Banks are interested in providing that capital with certain conditions. Primarily, they want to see other documentation as well as facts and figures to support your statement that the company is a good financial risk.

Bank financing, over the long haul, is usually the least expensive source of funds with the possible exception of government-supported loans. Unlike some other methods of raising capital, a bank loan won't require you to give anyone a share of the business. The bank's prime goal is to lend money to low-risk ventures and to make a profit for the shareholders of the bank.

Not all banks have the same loan programs. It's important that you investigate the financial institutions in your area and try to determine which ones specialize in providing small business loans. Some banks are closely affiliated with government small-business programs such as the Small Business Administration in the USA and the Small Business Loans Act in Canada.

Loans will be in the form of start-up capital or a working-capital line of credit. In most cases, banks will lend money for start-up capital to the value of your new equipment purchases and the cost of renovating your premises. The business owner would then be responsible to fund the start-up inventory costs.

Banks may also lend money to existing businesses against their accounts receivable, particularly if the company has a contract with a government department in the form of a standing purchase order. It's important, however, that copies of invoices and accounts-receivable records be supplied to the loans manager to show progressive billings with those contracts.

It is good business practice to maintain contact with bank officers. Communication on a weekly basis, by simply saying hello and telling them that the business is doing well, goes a long way to building up and maintaining their confidence in you. And, if you're experiencing a slow-down and sales are not up to your expectations, make an appointment to discuss matters with the manager. Being up-front with the bank about your problems, rather than having the banker find out from a third party, ensures a good relationship. Often, banks will offer some creative strategies to help you over the slow times.

It's almost essential to prepare monthly or, at a minimum, quarterly profit and loss statements to give to the bank. Include a short written report on how the business is doing, future work, work in progress, any major problems, and a general overview of the operation's progress based on your business plan forecasts. Remember, bankers deal in facts and figures, their skills are in accounting, not woodworking. If they believe your accounting procedures are first-rate, they'll be more comfortable.

And finally, nothing is more important to a banker than a good business plan. As previously stated, a well documented, accurately researched, and properly supported plan is absolutely necessary before banks will enter into any financial agreement with your new or existing business.

VENTURE CAPITAL

In cases where you can't secure bank financing, it may be necessary to seek other sources of capital. Venture financing is one option that might be considered. However, most venture capitalists will provide funds only in exchange for equity in the company. These lenders consider lending money to high-risk businesses, based on their opinion of the future prospects of that company. It can be more expensive than traditional bank financing and you must be prepared to give the investor a portion of the ownership of your company to secure the loan. But, it's sometimes better to retain a part of your business than none at all, if you can't raise capital in any other way.

Some venture capitalists are listed in directories available at public libraries. One source, entitled *Pratt's Guide to Venture Capital Sources,* is a well-known directory. Often, a short description in the directory gives details of the types of business investments that are of interest to the venture capital company. You can also find out about lenders in your area through accountants, lawyers and business brokers.

Venture capital funding is a world all its own and dealing with it can be complicated. Understanding the process usually means that you'll require the services of an accountant to determine if it's a viable option for you.

LONG-TERM DEBT

A loan, classified as long-term debt, is one form of initial financial arrangement that new small businesses should consider. The current month's interest, and a portion of the principal, are paid back to the lender on a monthly basis. The amount of the payment, as well as the loan term, is geared to the repayment ability of the new business.

Traditional sources for these business loans are commercial banks, government-sponsored programs, and small-business investment companies. Some new business owners have access to private loans from friends or relatives, which are repaid on a long-term debt basis.

LINES OF CREDIT

Securing a line of credit loan is a common form of borrowing money. It provides immediate short-term financing within a limit set by the bank. The company's credit line is used to pay its expenses until its accounts receivable generate a positive bank balance. Most credit line loans can be paid in full at any time and do not charge interest until funds are withdrawn. It's a useful form of financing for the small business owner because access to the money is immediate.

The bank manager will determine the value of your line of credit based on your business plan. Other debts, the company's ability to pay, and its sales history will be used in determining a value. It's well worth setting up a line of credit early, and increasing the limit as the business grows. Then, when that once-in-a-lifetime deal comes along, you'll have a ready source of cash.

LETTERS OF CREDIT

Letters of credit are guarantees that your bank will honor debts on your behalf. These letters will help you arrange credit with suppliers.

Many suppliers will request that a new business provide a letter of credit. The banks will review the supplier's request and determine the extent of their liability based on your business plan or on your past performance. If the bankers believe the risk is manageable, they will issue the letter to the supplier with a set dollar amount. The banks don't expect to pay the supplier. That's your responsibility, but the letter enables you to purchase stock on a 30-day credit term.

CHAPTER 4

LOCATION, LOCATION, LOCATION

We hear this phrase so often: "Location, Location, Location." Real estate agents would have us believe that they are the three most important factors for a successful business. And, while realtors do have a vested interest in that belief, there is a lot of truth in it. The business location, along with many other factors, does have an impact on sales.

The decision on where to locate is often governed by the cost of the space. While that is a valid reason, we must also look at the location's ability to generate client interest. The choice should be based on client-population density and ease of access, as well as proximity to your potential customers.

However, as woodworkers, we are at a disadvantage because of the noise and dust generated by our power tools. Some potential locations will be automatically ruled out, but we can't ignore the basic criteria when choosing a location just because of this disadvantage.

Make a decision before you start looking at potential locations. Do you need the customers traveling to your shop or will you conduct the major portion of your business dealings in the customer's home? Simply put, are they coming to you, or are you going to them? However, regardless of which scenario applies to you, try to pick a location that is close to your customer base.

TARGET MARKET

Your business plan should include information about your target market. Locating a kitchen cabinet shop in an area that has only new housing, for miles around your shop, won't be beneficial. You'll probably have a nice view, driving through a new subdivision each morning and evening, but you won't be building new kitchens there for many years to come.

As kitchen cabinetmakers, we conduct most of our business in the client's home. That will probably be a factor to weigh in making your decision. There is, however, value to be gained by having potential clients drive by your shop every day. A highly visible location will allow you to promote the business with store signs and window displays. Even simple, plain-looking industrial parks allow business signs. So, if you're locating in one of these areas and you have a choice, pick the store that is easily seen by passing motorists. Often, these parks front onto heavily traveled roadways where motorists have nothing else to do but look around while driving slowly in congested rush hour traffic.

POPULATION

Population density has two meanings that are important to your business. First, it means the number of people in a given area. And second, it's the number of people in a given area that could potentially be interested in your products.

We mentioned population in the overview chapter but, simply put, it's important to analyze factors such as the number of people in an area who may be interested in your products, what potential there is for growth of that population, and the number of similar businesses currently competing for the same client base.

Demographic research is a title used to mean analyzing the population's location and buying habits, the number of people per household, how many cars are owned by a family, and even the number of animals in a home. It can seem silly, but a simple statistic like the number of pets per household in a defined area is an extremely valuable piece of information for the person opening a new pet food store. The process involves selecting demographic information that is important to your business. Population density studies and other demographic databases are available from local and federal government branches. They are usually free for the new business owner and are a valuable resource.

ANALYZING THE AREA

A friend of mine recently opened a make-your-own wine store. His decision on location was based heavily on the population density near two potential buildings. He also researched the vehicle traffic flow by each site. He chose the store with the highest population density and traffic flow. It was also the most expensive location, nearly $3,000 per month, which was double the other store's rent.

I was surprised when he explained his reasons, and wondered if the expensive location was justified. However, he made the right decision because, at the end of his first year, his business was in a profitable position. His choice proved the value of location.

Look at the area before committing to the lease or purchase. Is it highly visible, clean and well kept, and are there established businesses in the area that will draw potential clients to your firm? For example, one business associate always tries to locate near beer and liquor stores. It's not his love for alcohol that influences him, but his belief that this type of business generates a lot of traffic. I don't know if there's any sense to that decision, but he always has a great deal of vehicle and pedestrian traffic going by his storefront on Saturdays.

In addition to traffic flow, consider your travel time. If your customer base is located far from the shop, a quick run back to the shop, or a sales call, can turn into hours of non-billable time. It's important to build a customer base close to the business location.

In the final analysis the choice of location should be based on many factors including:

1. How close is the shop to the potential client base?
2. The traffic flow, both vehicle and pedestrian.
3. Population density.
4. Access to the location by clients and staff.
5. The appearance of the area.
6. Shop viability.
7. The rules governing signs on the building.
8. Other businesses that will generate traffic.
9. The true cost of the property, including lease payments, percentage of sales commissions to the property owners, building maintenance fees, condominium charges if applicable, and utilities.
10. Ease of access and parking.

CHAPTER 5

SUPPLIERS

Suppliers can be either a never-ending source of problems or a great benefit to your business. A good supplier will offer quick service, good technical support, and a local supply inventory. For cabinet shops located in rural communities, choosing suppliers is even more important.

Kitchen cabinetmaking shops normally have two main suppliers, one providing hardware and another providing wood products. Both are essential to your business. Ideally, they will be located close to your shop and have knowledgeable salespersons .

These suppliers should sell only to the trade and should be classified as wholesalers. Buying your materials from companies that offer you retail prices doesn't give you any competitive advantage. Your bottom-line profit depends upon purchasing raw materials at the best possible price.

ESTABLISHING CONTACTS

In the early stages of setting up the business plan, research the wholesale distributors in your area. Speak to other business people who deal with those suppliers, so that you can determine the level of service offered by the distributors.

When you've narrowed the search to two or three companies, visit their stores. Speak to the staff concerning your intention to open a cabinetmaking business and find out what they have to offer. Pay attention to their attitude and the extent of their knowledge. Remember, in this case, you're the client, so don't hesitate to ask questions. If the wholesaler doesn't pay enough attention to your needs, take your business to another company.

If suppliers are in another city, or located far from your shop, it may be necessary to order by phone. In that case, you'll have to depend on transport companies to deliver the materials. However, make the initial contact with the supplier in person to establish the relationship. It's not hard to get badly-needed supplies delivered the next day by courier, but it's important to know that the supplier's staff understand your requirements. Many suppliers have representatives who travel from shop to shop. For the cabinet shop located in an area without a local supplier, a regular visit from a salesperson is an added bonus.

The cost price of materials is important but the level of service is equally important. I've often paid a few cents more for my hardware because of the extras I've received. When I need answers to technical questions about a product, I usually need the information quickly. Being ignored by the supplier, because I'm a small operator, may result in my losing work, and I don't believe we should have to put up with a lack of service and information from our wholesalers.

Just recently, a client inquired about the level of toxic emissions from a particular man-made wood product. I didn't have any idea that emissions were a problem, but this client had children who were allergic to specific toxins in some glues and didn't want to use them in his house. I called my supplier and had an answer in less than two hours in the form of a faxed data sheet. I gave my client a copy of the report and reviewed the results with him. Based on the speed of the reply and the attention to my client's needs, I was given the project even though my quote was a little higher than my competitor's. In effect, my supplier's attention to my request allowed me to get the contract. That was a lesson to me about the value of a supplier.

SETTING UP ACCOUNTS

Suppliers often open your account on a cash-only basis. This may continue for six months or until they feel comfortable with your ability to pay. From your perspective, the best situation is a 30-day account arrangement. You usually don't get paid in full from the client until you've completed the project, so having to pay in advance for hardware and materials reduces your available cash.

If your cash-flow situation is slow, you may need to draw on a credit line in order to pay for the raw materials. That situation adds to the wholesale cost of the products and reduces the profit

margin on the project. However, securing a letter of credit from your bank will allow the supplier to sell you goods on a 30-day basis. The supplier will give you a maximum credit limit equal to the value stated in the letter of credit.

Suppliers are vitally important to your business and you will naturally expect them to support your operation. But the reverse is also true. You should make every effort to pay the account on time, or even early if possible, because there is sometimes a discount for prompt payment. If suppliers have to keep calling you to try to get their money, they won't be too anxious to help you when you need them next.

My supplier's employees work hard. I'm sure that dealing with trade professionals like us, who want things done yesterday, can be tough. For that reason, I occasionally drop into their store with coffee and a box of doughnuts. It's my way of thanking them for their support. Such a simple way of saying thanks can go a long way toward cementing a strong working relationship between two companies. Your goodwill and show of appreciation will be rewarded.

CHAPTER 6

SETTING UP SHOP

Setting up your new shop involves more than merely finding the right place for a table saw. Your shop makes a statement to your customers about how well you're organized and how much you value your clients. Potential clients entering stores that look like the local junkyard won't feel good about spending their hard-earned cash.

Think about times when you've visited a home that was dirty, unorganized, and in bad need of repair. What were your impressions? It's a normal reaction to believe that the people who live there are dirty, disorganized, and don't really care about accomplishing very much. That may not always be true, but it's human nature to have those opinions.

Cabinet shops should be divided into two distinct areas: A work shop for cabinet production and a reception area for clients and staff. The workshop should be clean, well organized, and allow for maximum production with minimum effort. Reception areas should be quiet, well decorated and comfortable. A couple of coats of paint, a few plants, and some pleasant pictures are not expensive. First impressions are important.

It should be apparent to your customers that you are organized and that you and your staff have good work habits. In order to establish this impression, planning should begin early. Detail the ideal shop layout before you go looking for a location, so that you'll have an idea of the requirements. Once the choice is made, alter your plan to suit the location. Try to maintain the divided layout because, to many of your clients, a workshop with fancy tools means very little. On the other hand, some clients will be interested in seeing the workshop, particularly those who are weekend woodworkers themselves. Therefore, both reception area and shop should make positive statements about you and your business.

Does evidence of organization and cleanliness have an effect on the client? I really believe it does. For example, a friend of mine owns a small two-bay auto-repair business. He's been fixing my trucks for almost 15 years and I've built a few kitchens for him. Naturally, when people ask who I'd recommend to repair their car, I suggest my friend. After they have visited his shop, I often ask how the car is working. "Fine," they say. "He did a good job, but I can't get over how neat and tidy he keeps the garage. He cleans and puts all his tools in their place after every job, and the shop is spotless." They were more impressed with his clean, organized shop than with his repair work. Every time I hear comments about that small garage business, I am reminded of the importance of workshop organization, and the lasting impressions it creates.

Tip: TOOL FUND
Put away a small percentage of the revenue from each project billed as your tool fund. I try to add 3% to each project estimate to cover new tool purchases and replacement.

THE FLOOR PLAN

A floor plan that allows the cabinetmaker to work comfortably and quickly is a major asset to the business. We are constantly moving bulky cabinets and sheet goods during the production process, therefore, minimizing the effort means lessening fatigue and reducing the possibility of accidents.

Designing a workshop floor plan is a task that should be given a lot of attention. Think about all the steps required during one project and try to organize the process. The term that production planners use for this process is *workflow design.*

List all the steps required to build a kitchen cabinet. Consider all the moving and handling of materials, as well as each work station. For example, in my shop I store sheet goods and hardwoods near the table saw because that is the next step in the production process. I don't want to be moving materials any more than necessary, particularly heavy 4x8 sheets of $\frac{5}{8}$ in. melamine-coated particle core board.

As I cut the sheets into finished sizes, I stack them close to my assembly table so that it only takes a couple of steps to get the piece I need. Likewise, hardwood pieces are stored near the saw station and stacked beside the cut sheet goods. In my one-person shop, I do all the sanding, drilling and assembly on one table, so hardware and tool storage is located close to the table. Very little walking is needed in order to get all the parts and equipment for each cabinet.

The assembly table is located near the shop door, so that I can take the finished cabinets directly into the paint shop. A storage area for completed cabinets is located close to the finishing room, and that storage area has a shipping door from which I load the cabinets onto my truck. It's a simple process that avoids backtracking with materials or completed cabinets.

My shop isn't ideal. Most shops suffer from one problem or another because of space restrictions. It would be nice to have a 40-foot-wide by 200-foot-long shop with loading docks on each end. However, that is unrealistic. You will also have to make some adjustments to your ideal floor plan, but try to avoid unnecessary material handling.

TOOLS

Among cabinetmakers, there is an ongoing debate about which is more important, a table saw or a radial arm saw. Both are valuable pieces of equipment but, for the cabinet shop just starting up, difficult business decisions must sometimes be made as to which should be purchased first.

Tools for the production of cabinet doors will also be needed if you decide to build instead of buying pre-made. I don't believe it always makes economic sense to manufacture doors in a small kitchen cabinetmaking shop. However, I'll detail the basic equipment needed.

As your business grows, tools can be upgraded and faster production equipment can be easily purchased but, for the small shop starting out, here are the minimum requirements.

Basic Shop Equipment

1. 10-in. 3 HP table saw with sliding cross cut table
2. Drill press
3. 10 miter saw
4. Cordless screw gun
5. Heavy-duty router
6. Laminate trim router
7. Random orbit sander
8. Finish sander
9. Jig saw
10. Laminate rollers
11. Dust collector
12. Vacuum cleaner
13. Assorted pipe and bar clamps
14. Skill saw
15. Electric drill
16. Carbide router bits
17. Hand planer
18. Screwdrivers
19. Hand saws
20. Drill bits
21. Tables for cabinet assembly
22. Storage cabinets for tools and equipment

You'll also require all the basic shop supplies, including glue, sandpaper, cleaners and finishing goods such as paint brushes.

As the business grows you can add to the basic tool inventory in order to speed up production. These "nice to have" items include the following.

Additional Shop Equipment

1. Radial arm saw
2. Portable planer
3. Jointer
4. Bench router/shaper

5. Scroll saw
6. Cordless screw guns and drills
7. Biscuit joiner
8. HVLP finishing sprayer
9. Air compressor
10. Air brad and finishing nailers
11. Larger dust collector system
12. Additional clamps
13. Edge banders

Wood Cabinet-door Tools

1. Heavy-duty shaper
2. Stile and rail router bits
3. Power 24-inch belt sander
4. Clamp station

There is a never-ending assortment of hand and power tools that you'll need for specific applications. However, when I first started, I purchased only the basic tools and upgraded as the need arose. When I was hired for a project, I bought the tools that were needed to complete that job. In that way, I slowly added to my tool inventory.

Quality Tools

It's difficult to identify one or two manufacturers as the ultimate tool sellers. There are many excellent suppliers who take pride in their products and do their best to satisfy consumer requirements. Manufacturers such as Porter-Cable and Delta, as well as a few other old established firms,

Tip: BLADE CARE
A damaged or dull blade is dangerous. Take care of blades and sharpen them when necessary.

have proven their integrity in the marketplace. I use equipment from both companies extensively and have not had any major complaints.

One rule that I follow is to buy the best tool available within the budget allowed. As the old saying goes, "Buy the best and cry once; buy cheap and cry each time you use the tool."

For consumable equipment such as saw blades, drill bits, and router bits, carbide is the best option. High-speed steel bits will not last long when used for cutting high glue-content sheet goods and hardwoods. A high-quality carbide-tipped table saw blade can be sharpened many times before its useful life has ended. Be sure to use your saw blades properly. An 80-tooth 30-degree ATB blade, designed to cut plastic laminates, will be damaged if you use it to rip hard oak. Buy additional blades for specific uses in order to get the best quality cut.

Spend a little extra money for high-quality saw blades from companies such as FS Tool, Forrest, and Freud. Take time to investigate the saw-sharpening service providers in your area. It's to your advantage to deal with a sharpening service equipped with the latest computer-controlled equipment. Sharpening is an art and, if done properly, can extend the useful life of a blade for quite some time.

EQUIPMENT STORAGE

The woodworking portion of your shop should have a sufficient number of benches for assembly as well as proper storage compartments for tools.

Inexpensive plywood or particle board cabinets with doors will keep the dust off the cutting surfaces and out of the electrical motors of your equipment. One of your first projects should be the construction of these cabinets for your tools as well as for hardware items such as screws, nails, glues and cleaners.

Easy-to-read labels on parts drawers will help speed up the cabinet-construction process, because you can find what you're looking for immediately, and you can tell at a glance when stock is running low.

Organizing the workshop relates directly to the efficiency of production, and that efficiency has a direct impact on the bottom line. Waste time during assembly, or spoil a can of contact cement, and you let a few more dollars disappear from the shop's net profit.

PRODUCT DISPLAY

Product display, in most small shops, is located in the reception area. We usually have upper and lower cabinets with several door styles and accessories to show our clients. Hardware, brochures, and other company literature, along with pictures of completed projects, often fill the available space. It's an expensive use of floor area, as it takes away from production space, but it is necessary for generating sales. Many small shops also utilize the reception space for desks and filing cabinets.

It's particularly important that this display area be neat and tidy. The room should be well lit and all products should be arranged for easy access by your clients. Flood or spot lighting can be used to focus attention on your cabinet work. Design the setting to duplicate an actual kitchen environment as closely as possible. If clients can easily visualize your cabinets in their kitchen, you have already accomplished half the work of selling that client. If your desk must be located in the showroom, try to keep it as neat and unobtrusive as possible.

CLIENT COMFORT

Some cabinetmaking shops depend on traffic flow for exposure and the owners expect clients to visit their showroom. If you're fortunate enough to locate in a highly visible area, you can count on people dropping by your shop.

Once prospective customers have walked in the door, make their visit as comfortable as possible. Well-placed chairs, quiet surroundings, and maybe a cup of coffee, can help to make a customer more receptive to your sales efforts. Details that we often overlook, such as clean washrooms, room temperature, and use of the display area as a staff shortcut, detract from client comfort. One company's slogan states: "Customers are our most important asset." It's a saying that's worth remembering.

CHAPTER 7

ADVERTISING AND MARKETING

The most successful cabinetmakers are good at what they do, and good at telling others what they do. Both skills have to be mastered, that of the artisan and that of the communicator. A self-employed cabinetmaker has to use communication skills to tell people about the high quality produced by the artisan. There are only certain individuals who need our services, however, and they are the target market. Our challenge is to reach the target market in the most efficient and effective way possible.

The most crucial element in your marketing plan is defining and identifying this target group. There are some people who obviously don't need our services, such as the kids at the local day care center. Posting flyers on the center's bulletin won't do you a lot of good. Or will it? What about the parents who pick up the children? This example is a little farfetched, but it illustrates how subtle the marketing process can be.

A certain amount of research will have been completed in the business plan. It now requires an exhaustive study. You need to develop a marketing plan. One question should be at the top of your plan: Who is the target market?

In the initial stages of developing a marketing plan, look to the obvious groups, the ones least expensive to reach. Usually, they will be the homeowners in the general area of your shop. Analyze each section of the area. Are there older homes in one part, a new subdivision in another section, or a mix of old and new developments? Divide the area by type, and target the most likely people. For the kitchen cabinetmaker, it will probably be owners of older homes, as they are the mostly likely candidates for new cabinets.

Once the target group is defined, develop a marketing strategy. What products are you going to feature? How are you going to reach these potential clients? And, what is your pricing strategy? Keep in mind the four factors that your marketing strategy addresses: Product, promotion, distribution and price.

A marketing plan also accounts for the competition in your area. Who are they? How does their business operate? What are their strengths and weaknesses? And how do their products compare with yours? I find it helpful to keep a record of all comments I hear and information that I learn about my competitors. I use a different notebook for each of my competitors. If I'm visiting someone's home, I ask who built the kitchen and I record the conversation if it happens to be a competitor in my area. If possible, I'll look at the work performed, noting the good and bad features. It's a basic business principal: The best tool in your shop is information.

I don't believe in meeting the competitor's price every time. However, it is necessary to know what they are charging. You may decide your shop's quality is superior, or you're offering more than just a cabinet, to justify your higher retail pricing. If you plan on marketing by this value-added philosophy, be certain that your reasons are obvious to the customers. In your advertising, play up the bonus features. You might say something like, "We may be a little higher priced, but quality costs a little more." Stress the good points such as better quality hardware, thicker carcass material, full cabinet backs, custom designing and so on. Put the questions on the table during sales presentations by telling the customer that your prices are higher for some very good reasons. Most customers will buy quality if they feel they're getting value for their money. Design a brochure showing the value-added features in big bold type and leave a copy of the brochure after every sales call. The customer will then have your brochure for reference when evaluating all the quotes.

Advertising is the life blood of every business. Without it, you may as well stay at home. But remember that as cabinetmakers, we're not just selling a product, we're selling ourselves. The sales effort involves advertising, personal contacts, and promotion. To consumers, a gallon of fuel is simply that. They use it and get more. Cabinetmaking, to the consumer, involves not only the cabinet but also, more importantly, the person who builds it. It's a major investment for a product that will be used each and every day. We really do have to sell our integrity.

NEWSPAPERS

The local newspaper is an excellent way to get out a general message that you're in business. Display advertising can be expensive, however, so if your budget is limited, consider advertising in the classified section. Often, newspapers have a reasonably-priced homeowner's service directory in or near their classified section.

Advertising in newspapers allows you to get your name out to the public. Ads are normally structured to attract attention in a general sense such as: "Bob's Kitchen Cabinetmaking. High Quality Cabinets at Reasonable Prices." Specific products are featured when you have a product or service on special. It may be something like "20% Off All Wood Kitchen Cabinets Until Christmas. Call Bob's Kitchen Cabinetmaking."

It's possible to get free advertising from newspapers, especially small local papers, by sending them your press releases. Submitting well written, one-page press releases to the newspaper's editorial department can attract a lot of attention when the subject is interesting. A typical press release might read: "Bob's Kitchen Cabinetmaking, located in Smalltown, has been awarded a contract to build kitchen cabinets for Sleepy Nursing Home in Bigtown."

Send the notice to various newspapers on your company letterhead. Type "PRESS RELEASE" in the upper lefthand corner. Type "FOR IMMEDIATE RELEASE" in the upper righthand corner with the date, contact name and phone numbers below.

In the center of the page, type your information, double spaced. Keep the information short and to the point. In the first paragraph, describe the "who, what, where, when and why," the five Ws of press reporting. In the second paragraph, include details about the current project that will be of interest to the reader. In the third paragraph, supply background information on your business and its personnel.

One page is enough, as most editors won't publish a long, drawn-out story unless their reporters have written it. The article should be news: short and sweet. Review some press releases that have already been used by the local papers. Analyze how they're structured so that you have a feel for the type of release most likely to get published.

Look around your business for interesting information. It's surprising how much newsworthy material is available for free press release advertising. Possibly you've agreed to represent a different cabinet door company, have an interesting new line of kitchen accessories, or are the only one in town certified to install a new line of solid-surface countertop material. If one of your customers says, "That's interesting," think about what they've found interesting, and why. It might make a good press release.

DIRECT MAIL

Direct mail is my preferred method of advertising. Once I've established a target group, I prepare an information flyer and mail it to those people. Usually, the target group is a well-defined area of homes in a part of town that is most likely in need of my services.

One advantage that technology offers are mailing lists by area, name, phone number and postal code, for every city in North America. They are available on CD-ROM and allow you to search and create a mailing list for specific areas. The program that I have will print the lists directly onto self-adhesive mailing labels. And, each year, the software company releases an updated version of the program with all the latest changes.

You can also purchase mailing lists from publications, such as magazines that cater to your target groups. These lists can be separated by postal code or city. Some of these magazines are very focused, for example a publication specializing in kitchens and baths, and have recent, up-to-date lists.

FLYERS

Distributing advertising flyers to a neighborhood is also an effective way to generate business. This method of advertising is not as targeted as direct mail, but it's much less expensive. Some local post offices will distribute these flyers in predetermined postal walks, or you can hire students to do the job.

Most people will only glance at a flyer they consider junk mail unless it catches their interest. Therefore, it's important that the message be simple, direct and easy to read. Flyers are particularly useful when you have a special offer. Printing sale details on brightly colored paper will grab the reader's attention.

BUSINESS CARDS

Business cards are the most under-used form of advertising, which is surprising when you realize how little they cost. One thousand cards cost about $20. They don't have to be fancy: Name, address and phone number are sufficient when combined with a short, snappy phrase that sums up your message.

Many people are hesitant to give out business cards, and I don't understand why. I order them by the thousand and leave them everywhere. When I pay business and personal bills, I include a card. If I'm in a restaurant, I leave a card on the table with the tip. Whenever I have to leave a note for someone, it's written on the back of my card. The more you use your business card, the more chances you will have to develop new business. If a thousand cards are thrown away and only one gets me a new client, that card order has more than paid for itself.

Set a goal to give away ten cards a day. It may be difficult at first, but soon you'll find it a natural part of your business day. Spending 20 dollars to have 1000 potential customers read your message is an inexpensive form of advertising.

SIGNS

There are three types of signs commonly used in the cabinetmaking business. The first is the one on your shop. It should be large, well lit, kept in good repair, and carry a message that quickly tells the client what you do. If your shop is located in an area that has a high traffic flow, make sure the sign is visible from the roadway. Passing motorists have only about one second in which to read the message, so make it effective.

The second type of sign advertising is on your truck. It's a silent salesperson when you travel. If possible, drive your truck instead of an unmarked

vehicle, even when you're not working. A Saturday trip to the grocery store means that your signs are visible to shoppers while you're getting groceries. At the children's baseball game, all the parents will see your advertising and you don't have to say a word. I drive my company truck everywhere, even to church.

Because this sign is so visible, and because it's moving throughout the city every day, a lot of thought should be given to its design. Again, like the store sign, it should be simple and effective. Put the company name, general location and phone number in large letters with a small message such as *We build quality kitchens*. On most trucks, you have the two sides plus the tailgate for your advertising copy. I'm still working on how to put a sign on the front of my truck.

Third is the project-site sign. Often, it's a two-sided sign that can support itself. Such sandwich boards are placed on the lawn or sidewalk when a cabinetmaker is installing a kitchen at a client's home. Neighbors like to see what's going on in their neighborhood, so this is an ideal opportunity to get free advertising and possibly land another job in the area. Simple and direct, with easy-to-read type, is always the best policy with signs and this one is no exception. It can read: *Another Quality Kitchen Project by Bob's Cabinet Shop. Phone 123-4567.* If the neighbors don't phone you right away, they'll at least make it a point to talk to your client and ask about the new kitchen.

Site signs are powerful messages. Most people think that because your company was good enough for their neighbor, it's good enough for them. In an older townhouse row, I started by completing one kitchen and ended up building six more over the next two years. The total cost of the advertising was the time it took me to put my site sign on the lawn at each townhouse.

THE PRESENTATION ALBUM

There are two methods by which we can effectively use photographs of completed projects. The first is a display album of all our completed kitchens, which we show to prospective clients. This album should also contain letters of reference, clippings of press releases, and information on the types of hardware and materials we used, as well as pictures of special accessories. You'll close more sales using a high-quality photo album than by any other method. It's an important sales tool, so the album should be of the highest quality: If you know very little about photography, taking a night course will pay many dividends.

Everyone likes to look at pictures. When I open my album, the potential customer's whole family crowds around to have a look. You'd wonder why a six year old wants to look at photos of kitchens until you realize it's the pleasure of looking at pictures in an album that interests people of all ages. I've sometimes seen it get to the point where the client's children are fighting over my album.

Take pictures for the presentation album after the project has been completed. When the film is taken for processing, order two sets of prints, one to use in your advertising and the other for a special customer album, a small pocket-sized album

with a thank-you note and business card on the inside front cover. I place the best overall kitchen photo the first page opposite the card and the note, then mail the album with a covering letter to my client. It's a simple way to say thanks for the business but, more importantly, it's another form of advertising.

Most clients are proud of their new kitchens. They've probably talked about the project to friends, neighbors and coworkers for the past six months. Now, they have photographs of the completed project to show them. When the album is opened, the first page displays the business card and thank-you note. I've gained more new clients from this kind of promotion than from any other form of advertising. It's an extremely effective sales tool and the cost is minimal, just a few dollars for the prints and a few more for the album.

WORD OF MOUTH

As kitchen cabinetmakers, we have one powerful resource that is sometimes ignored and that is our client-base of completed projects. Don't underestimate the value of your past customers. Each time you complete a project for a fully-satisfied client, you add one more spokesperson representing your company.

With a few exceptions, it's in your best interest to make sure the client is pleased with your work. But there is the rare occasion when you simply can't satisfy a client. It seems that no matter what you do, they aren't happy. I've had the odd person like this, as I'm sure every other businessperson has had as well, but I'll do everything possible to try to satisfy the client, even to the point of reducing my profit to zero if absolutely necessary.

Why go to these extremes? Well, word-of-mouth advertising, when generated by a client who has used your services, can be the one of the most powerful forms of advertising you'll encounter. Nothing is more effective than someone saying, "I've used Bob's Cabinet Shop and it was the best decision I've ever made. Bob and his crew were great." It doesn't matter if your prices are a little higher, when a potential client hears a personal endorsement of your shop, your name will be remembered.

LETTERS OF REFERENCE

After completing a project, speak to your client and verify that everything was done satisfactorily. If the customer is happy, don't hesitate to ask for a letter of reference. These letters, whether a formally typewritten document or a signed hand-written note, speak louder than any form of advertising you could design yourself. Place the letters in the front of your photographic presentation album so that they'll be easily seen by a prospective client. It's not necessary to say anything further. New clients will naturally read these letters and form positive opinions of your shop's credibility.

When submitting a quotation, include two or three copies of the best letters as attachments. Not many contractors do this. They add a line in their quote stating, "Letters of reference on request." Don't wait to be asked. Many new clients are hesitant to request letters of reference, so let them know that your work is excellent and that your previous customers have supported you with written statements.

RAISING YOUR PERSONAL PROFILE

Cabinetmakers must sell themselves. Personal integrity and quality of work are of equal importance but, when you're unknown, when you maintain a low profile and remain hidden away in your shop, nobody is able to form an opinion of your character.

Do you want to be well-known and, at the same time, do something good for others? Join one of the local service clubs or participate as a coach in the minor sports leagues in your area. You'll get a lot of satisfaction from being a community-minded citizen and you'll raise your personal profile in the process. Meeting new people and renewing old acquaintances is known as *networking* and offers many rewards from both a personal and a business point of view.

CHAPTER 8

ESTABLISHING THE WORKFORCE

There are many details to remember if you plan to hire employees. As an employer, you must be aware of the wage- and hours-of-work laws in your area. You must make employee deductions and remit those funds to the appropriate government departments. There are details regarding worker's accident insurance and regulations to learn, and many other forms, regulations, bylaws, federal and local issues that you must understand as an employer. Ignorance of the law will not often be accepted as an excuse.

Hiring and paying employees is a lot more complicated than merely issuing a check every two weeks. The time and money involved, for you or for your bookkeeper, is a major consideration but, if you want to operate as a medium-sized cabinet shop, employees are a necessity.

There are also the matters of insurance, worker's compensation legislation, and workplace health and safety laws. Don't forget, also, liability insurance covering your business and covering any situations that you or your employees cause which may be considered as damage to another person or their property. Business insurance policies also cover fire, theft, and accident to clients or employees.

BUSINESS STYLE

You can operate your business as a sole proprietorship, partnership, limited or incorporated company. Business descriptions and operating style terminology differ slightly from area to area but, basically, a sole proprietorship means you own the business as the only shareholder, while a partnership means that both you and your business partner are registered owners. A limited or incorporated company is a little more complicated, but incorporation does offer provisions for limiting your personal liability.

There are tax laws and implications appropriate to each business style. It's a worthwhile exercise to investigate all the pros and cons of each. I suggest you get all the regulatory information for all business styles that are applicable to your area, then meet with an accountant to discuss which form of business registration best suits your needs.

Deciding on which form of business you want to operate should be one of your early considerations, but you should also plan for the future. You may want to start off operating as a one-person shop with expansion possible in the near future. Therefore, it may be in your best interests to register as a limited company to allow for those plans. Again, an accountant can advise you on all the alternatives, based on your future business plans.

PART-TIME AND FULL-TIME STAFF

Staffing can be a major source of frustration. As any business owner knows, you have more to gain and more to lose than your employees have, so you need a total commitment to the business.

Your staff won't have that same level of dedication. Most employees will do a good job and will be interested in your success but they can take their pay checks, go home at the end of the day, and not have to worry about the business. You, however, will be thinking about the operation night and day.

What type of employer-employee relationship is best for you? That depends, to a large extent, on your business style. A sole proprietor may only need staff on a part-time basis to help with cutting sheet goods and installing cabinets. If you are planning a larger operation, staffing may be an important issue.

TRAINING

It doesn't matter whether your staff members work full time or part time, some training will be necessary and the cost of that training can be expensive. If they're trained on the job or in the shop, you'll have to devote a certain amount of your own productive time to instructing new employees.

You may have to hire two or three people in succession until you find that one person whose abilities and interest level are just right for you. This turnover can be a big investment for shops with several employees, but of course you must have qualified people whom you can trust to complete their tasks to your standards.

For those shops that use part-time help, it is sometimes difficult to provide enough work to keep employees busy. Often, part-timers have other jobs and this may require you to schedule your

own production to coincide with their availability. Most shops, including mine, have a number of trained part-time employees they can call when necessary. It often means trying to divide the work so that each gets a share, but if that's the way your shop operates, you don't have many options.

Employing full-time staff is easier when it comes to dividing the workload. The employees are in the shop every day, so you don't have to be concerned about their availability. However, when business is slow, you do have to continue to pay your staff. One way or another, employee management can be time-consuming.

How to build a kitchen cabinet

Trade School Resources

If you're fortunate enough to live in an area where there is a trade school or college, you may have a source of trained personnel available. Some schools operate a work-placement program with students going to work in private industry to gain practical experience. If you can register as a work-placement employer, you may be able to get temporary, reasonably well-trained staff, often at reduced labor rates.

Government-sponsored Programs

Government employment centers, and programs created by the government to help train people in various trades, can be another source of low cost labor. Inquire at the local employment or unemployment center (government employment programs have different names in different areas) to find out how your company can participate.

Hiring government-sponsored employees can be financially beneficial to a new business. Training time is reduced and often the hourly wage of those employees is subsidized by the government. You get the best of two worlds, an eager, interested employee at a reduced cost, but keep in mind that these people are only on temporary loan to your business. However, it does allow you to evaluate different people and you may find ideal employees who will work for you when they graduate from the program.

CHAPTER 9

ACCOUNTING

Accounting means much more than writing down which bills to pay and the amount of money coming into the business. It means good recordkeeping for every transaction that takes place. It is necessary to be aware of your profit-and-loss position at all times.

Accurate records are required by each level of government. Banks and lenders also need this information and, most importantly, you must be constantly informed of the health of the business if you are to succeed.

There are many accounting systems. Some are manual and others are computer-based. It's not important which you prefer, as long as the resulting records are accurate. Analyzing the business plan every month or every quarter is only possible if all transactions are recorded.

Here are some basic housekeeping rules for the small business:

1. Record all transactions.
2. Open a business account at the bank.
3. Pay business bills by check whenever possible.
4. Deposit sales income as soon as possible.
5. Reconcile your bank account monthly.
6. Set up a petty-cash float, but use it only when absolutely necessary.
7. Keep and record all receipts.
8. Order goods/materials on a purchase-order form.
9. Set-up a monthly inventory record.
10. Assign folders and files for all records.

There are many more good recordkeeping practices that can be applied specifically to your business. The goal is to maintain accurate, easily-accessible information so that you know the financial position of your business at all times. If and when trouble comes, there are some positive steps you can take in order to turn things around, but first you must be well-informed. We'll cover the question of corrective action later in this section.

YOUR FINANCIAL ADVISOR

Using the services of an accountant or a well-versed business manager/bookkeeper is a necessity because there are so many rules, regulations, financial programs, and monthly reports which are often beyond the skills of the average business person. After all, our own task is to create a product for sale, not to become financial or business management experts. However, some basic financial skills are an absolute necessity. The most important of these is knowing when our own abilities are limited and who to hire.

Accountants' skills are in financial and business management matters. That's their field of expertise. It makes good business sense to meet with an accountant when you're creating a business plan, seeking financing or making a complicated financial decision, but it is equally important to talk to the accountant on a regular basis in order to analyze the state of your business

Most accounting firms will discuss ahead of time the level to which they should be involved, the cost of their services, and what they can do for your business. During the first meeting, explain your requirements and ask for an estimate. This is an acceptable practice and most accountants appreciate being able to go over these matters at the start of your association with their firm. That way, there won't be any misunderstandings or surprises later.

ACCOUNTS RECEIVABLE

Accounts receivable are the accounts you have invoiced that are unpaid: The money generated by your sales that is still owed to your business. How do you manage this financial area? Simply, collect all the money owing as quickly as possible. That's the easy answer, but it is not always possible to collect outstanding accounts immediately.

Cash flow is determined by comparing the amount of money spent with the amount of money collected. Positive cash flow means there is more money coming in than going out. Negative cash flow is the opposite. When in a negative position, the business must draw on reserve funds, or even borrow, in order to meet its obligations.

A big part of any business is managing the accounts receivable. One way to lessen the burden is to develop an operating formula for collecting money. Cabinetmakers have one business advantage because most of their projects are large. For the kitchen cabinetmaker, that usually means

billing a project worth a few thousand dollars. Many make it a requirement that the client pay a set percentage of the contract at the time of signing. Further, many cabinetmakers, including myself, inform the client that the balance is due at the time of completion.

It's not uncommon, when building cabinets for a kitchen renovation project, to spend 30% of the project's retail value on materials. As most cabinet projects are designed specifically for a particular client, I don't believe it's unreasonable to ask for a 50% down payment when the contract is signed. If the situation arises where the client can't or won't pay, at least the cost of materials, and a portion of other shop expenses, are covered by the deposit.

I believe it's important to be candid with clients. We agree to give them everything they've contracted for, and sometimes more. Customers should therefore understand, and agree to keep, their part of the contract. Write down all the specifics in the contract and make the client aware of the terms. On the line where the customer signs, type: "It is agreed that we will pay 50% of the purchase price at the time of signing and the balance on completion of the project." This is plain and simple, and leaves no chance for a misunderstanding.

It should be understood that we all have to invest a considerable amount of money in order to realize a small profit. That's normal with most businesses. If you can't collect on one of your projects, much of the net profit for the next few jobs will be needed to recover from that bad debt. It's one of the major reasons why good accounts-receivable management is crucial.

Proper management of accounts receivable is only possible through accurate recordkeeping. The cost of overdue accounts compounds daily, particularly if you have to borrow money to meet expenses. Before you realize what has happened, the profit from the overdue account is zero. Let the overdue account run any longer and it's costing you money.

DISASTER-RECOVERY PLANNING

Being in a negative-cash-flow situation means using up any surplus money that has been accumulated in the business. When that runs out, you must borrow from the bank. When loans are no longer available, and you can't meet expenses, the business will soon fail.

There are early warning signs that should cause you to take a long, hard look at your financial situation. When you are unable to take advantage of a supplier's early-payment discounts because you haven't got ready cash on hand, you should think about the reasons for it. When you suffer a lack of business for an extended period of time, ask yourself why. If you're using a personal line of credit to the maximum limit, and find it difficult to pay bills and expenses on time, you have an obvious problem with your cash flow.

The first way to avoid some of these problems is to complete a monthly profit and loss statement. Don't wait to see what happens next month, take positive action now. A negative cash-flow situa-tion can often be corrected by reducing the value of your accounts receivable. If your customers aren't paying you, you cannot pay your suppliers.

Second, try to reduce expenses to those that are absolutely necessary to the growth and maintenance of the operation. Get rid of all your extras, at least temporarily. Next, complete any outstanding work so that your clients will pay your invoices. Increasing your sales is the immediate goal, so concentrate on closing outstanding work, then follow up sales leads that might generate work. Leave other things aside and concentrate on being a salesperson.

Discuss the situation with your bank manager. Let him or her know that you are having a little difficulty and outline the steps you are taking to correct the situation. Ask for advice and make the business records available to the bank.

If the situation continues to get worse, talk to your suppliers to try to reduce payments with extended terms. If you've been in business for a while and have kept your account in good standing, they will usually accommodate your request. They don't want to lose a good customer.

If the corrective action isn't immediate successful, consider selling some of the assets in your business to help the situation. Possibly there's an extra truck or table saw that is not critical to the business that, when sold, will raise cash. Above all, don't give up. It's usually a minor downturn in the economy that affects most businesses. If you have a good plan and stay on top of the cash flow you'll recover.

CHAPTER 10

KITCHEN DESIGN AND CABINETRY

Nothing is more disruptive to a family's lifestyle than a major kitchen renovation project. Most family members spend a great deal of their time in the kitchen. The kitchen is used for meal preparation, for informal eating and for casual gatherings. People soon realize how important that room is when it's torn apart during renovations, when making a cup of coffee becomes a major undertaking. It is therefore critically important that the tear-out and the new installation are coordinated properly in order to minimize down-time. If you want a real-life drama, tell a family that their kitchen will be down another week because you forgot to order something, or because your dimensions were wrong and you have to rebuild a cabinet.

Most experts agree that a kitchen renovation project will return almost 100% on investment when the property is sold. Surveys by the real estate industry show that a kitchen is one of the features considered first by potential purchasers. Real estate agents have told me that the quality of the kitchen often makes or breaks a sale.

Kitchen design is a critical phase of any kitchen cabinetmaking renovation project.

Kitchen design is subjective. A feature or layout that is perfect for one person is far from perfect for another. Each family's lifestyle and how that lifestyle involves the kitchen is unique to that household. In most cases the family, as primary users of the kitchen space, will have definite ideas on what is needed and what the end result has to be in order to meet their needs. Often, you'll find that they have been looking through magazines, drawing rough floor plans, measuring, and dreaming about their ideal kitchen for quite some time.

During my first visit with clients, I find that my role is that of a provider of information about new products and features on the market. I ask questions about clients' requirements and ideas, then take their responses and their rough drawings, with my own accurate measurements, back to the shop so that I can come up with two or three different floor plans. I try not to radically alter major features my clients want, but I will suggest alternatives if I see something unsafe or poorly designed, while trying to incorporate their most important ideas into my various plans.

A cabinetmaker should ask questions in order to understand all the client's needs. Consultants call this a needs-analysis study, and although I don't go in for fancy titles, I think the term applies in this case. Some of the areas that should be covered are listed in the next column:

1. Discuss the existing kitchen space and layout with the client, listing the good and bad points of the design as seen by the client.

2. Investigate the traffic patterns in and through the kitchen.

3. Analyze the day-to-day meal preparation tasks. Try to understand the family's normal daily meal preparation routine.

4. Questions should be asked about the client's desire to do more in the kitchen. Would the family spend more time on a hobby such as baking, or other areas of interest, if the kitchen offered added space or facilities?

5. Does the client move around the kitchen alot during meal preparation?

6. Ask whether or not cleaning up after meals seems to be a monumental task. You may not solve that problem completely, but clean-up time could be reduced by simple layout changes.

7. Perhaps your customer would like to do more entertaining in the kitchen, or would like to serve more formal meals in the dining room, if the functionality of the kitchen space could be improved.

8. Determine how long your clients plan to own the house. A $20,000 kitchen renovation may not be fully recoverable if the intention is to upgrade for a quick sale in the near future. If you convince someone to over-improve, and the return is not realized during resale, you will have lost a client who might otherwise provide a referral.

9. Discuss the client's wish list. If space and money were no object, what would the clients like to have in their dream kitchen?

10. Discuss topics such as lighting, both area and task illumination, and kitchen seating needs, as well as appliance upgrade needs.

Other areas of concern may become evident during your visit. I've found that listening closely and asking a lot of questions is the best approach. I try to imagine myself as the client and to see things from that perspective.

Kitchen design is a difficult process because everyone's needs and desires are different. I've designed and built cabinets and work spaces that I wouldn't have in my own kitchen, and I'm sure the reverse is equally true: My clients might not like my family's kitchen at all. Kitchen design is based on personal and individual tastes.

Two design rules that seem to be true in every case, however, deal with color and illumination. Light color or natural wood cabinets can brighten and visually enlarge a space. Improved general lighting and task lighting will always enhance the project. Some older kitchens have dark cabinets combined with poor illumination, which gives everyone the impression of being in a cave. Yesterday's kitchen was simply a place in which to prepare the meal and clean up. Today's lifestyle is often focused on the kitchen as a gathering place for a wide and varied number of activities, therefore the room has to be bright, seem large, be functional, and adapt to many of those activities.

There are many styles of layouts including the L-shaped kitchen, galley kitchen, U-shaped kitchen and island style. However, most kitchen designers agree that the sum of all the legs in a work triangle in any kitchen (the triangle from the refrigerator to the stove to the sink and back to the refrigerator) should not be less than 10 feet or greater than 25 feet. If the sum of the legs in the work triangle is too small, people will be tripping over each other. If it is too large, food preparation may be a tiring task. I analyze this work pattern every time I design a kitchen layout and the analysis has proven to be valuable.

If you feel intimidated by the kitchen design process, you may want to investigate the possibility of enrolling in design courses offered by community colleges in your area. Look into the availability of seminars offered by local, provincial/state, and federal trade associations. There is a National Kitchen and Bath Association listed in the phone book of most large cities that may have information on courses or seminars available to you.

Kitchen design is so important that there is a Kitchen Designer certification program. People who are certified usually specialize exclusively in this area, which shows me just how large and how important the kitchen renovation field has become. There is a good living to be made, with a great deal of job satisfaction, in the kitchen ren-

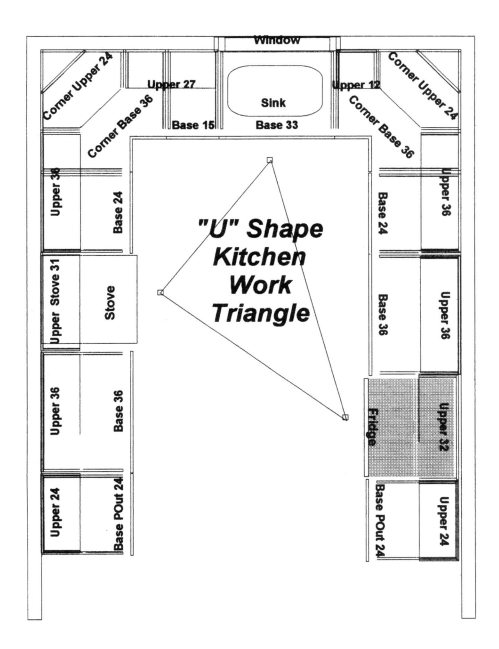

Window

Corner Upper 24

Upper 27

Corner Upper 24

Upper 12

Corner Base 36

Sink

Corner Base 36

Base 15

Base 33

Upper 36

Base 24

Base 24

Upper 36

**"U" Shape
Kitchen
Work
Triangle**

Upper Stove 31

Stove

Base 36

Upper 36

Upper 36

Base 36

Upper 24

Base POut 24

Fridge

Upper 32

Base POut 24

Upper 24

Figure 10-2
A U-shaped kitchen design, showing the work triangle. This style presents some interesting problems in design because entry into the room is limited to one path. Often, there is only one window, which determines the placement for the kitchen sink. The stove and refrigerator should be placed so that more than one person can work in the kitchen without getting in the way of one another.
Drawing courtesy of Quisine Insite Kitchen Drawing Software

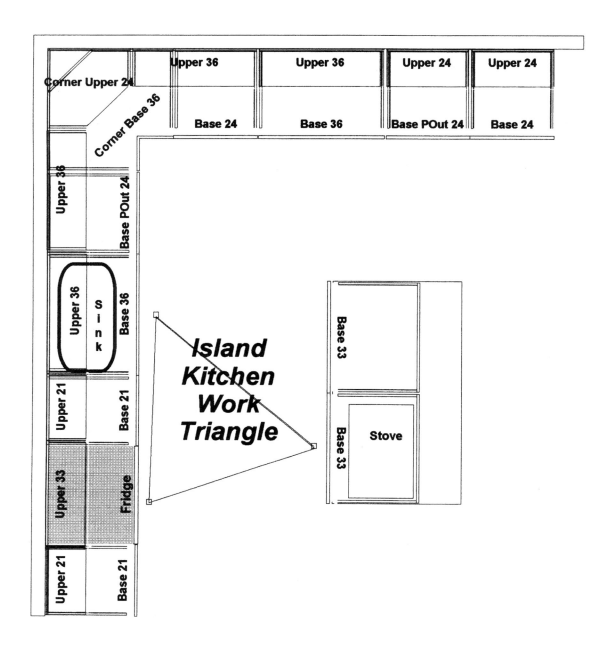

Figure 10-3
An island or L-shaped kitchen, showing the work triangle. An island added to a simple L-kitchen transforms the room into a dynamic work space.
Drawing courtesy of Quisine Insite Kitchen Drawing Software

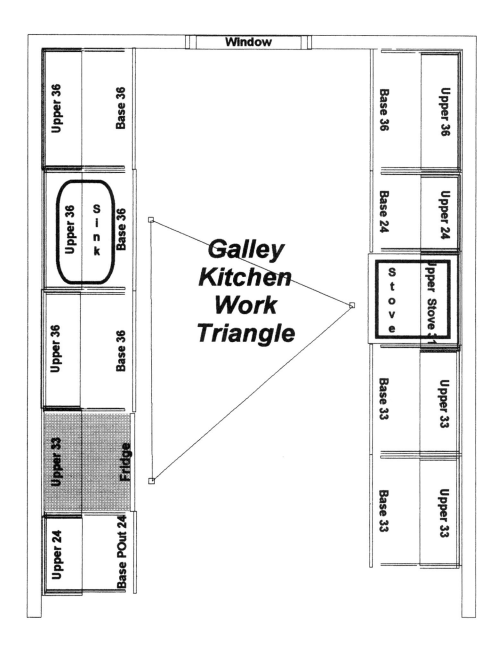

Figure 10-4
The galley kitchen, showing the work triangle. Traffic flow through the room can cause accidents in kitchens with this design. When the galley kitchen is open at both ends, pay special attention to the family's need to use this room to gain access to other areas of the house. High traffic means special consideration is required for appliance door swings and cooking requirements. Crossing a highly-used traffic area, while carrying pots of hot liquid, can be extremely dangerous. If this is a common practice, modifications such as locating the stove and sink on the same side might be worth considering.
Drawing courtesy of Quisine Insite Kitchen Drawing Software

ovation field. As in all specialized trades, the greatest teacher is experience, but I still buy and read every book I see on kitchen cabinetmaking and design. I strongly suggest that you read books, attend seminars and training programs, and analyze every kitchen you see for ideas and techniques.

CABINET DESIGN

Two designs of kitchen cabinets will be described in this manual. The first is the face-frame cabinet.

The traditional North American style of kitchen cabinet is basically a box with a wooden face frame attached to the front edge. Doors are installed so that they overlap the face frame with

a space between cabinet doors. Most designs use an exposed hinge and center stile.

Traditional cabinets were supported on a wooden base with end cabinet sides (gable ends) extended to the floor. Often, the drawers were supported on wooden runners or tracked in grooves on the drawer box.

Early traditional North American cabinets were frame-and-panel construction, using glued up boards for the sides, backs, and bottoms. And, most often, the cabinets were built in place.

The European frameless kitchen cabinet consists of a box, usually made from laminate-coated par-

Figure 10-5
The North American style face-frame cabinet is a popular choice.

Figure 10-6
The European style frameless cabinet on the right, compared to a
more traditional North American cabinet on the left.

ticle core board. The edges of the box are taped with plastic edge tape or have high-pressure laminate applied. Doors are a particle core board with high-pressure laminate.

The Europeans have developed the adjustable cabinet base leg to replace the wooden base support. A hidden, three-way adjustable hinge is also used, eliminating the need for a cabinet center stile. Drawer glides of metal, attached to the cab-

inet gable ends and drawer bottom, are a European standard.

European cabinetry depends in part on the high-quality European door hinge and its ability to adjust in three directions. The quality of this hinge allows for accurate placement of the cabinet doors because of the hinge's mechanical ability to hold that placement. Because the European hinge was developed for, and is almost exclusively used on, European-style cabinetry, or cabinets without the traditional North American face frame, hinge styles are named in reference to the European cabinet. A full-overlay European hinge is meant to fully cover or overlay the gable end edge of the cabinet. Carcass thickness is normally $\frac{5}{8}$ in., so a full-overlay European hinge covers approximately $\frac{5}{8}$ in. of the cabinet face. I say "approximately," because metric measure is widely used with these hinges, as they are European-based, and there is a slight difference. However, for our purposes we can assume a full-overlay hinge covers $\frac{5}{8}$ in. of the cabinet face and a half-overlay hinge covers approximately $\frac{5}{16}$ in. of the face.

The high quality of this hinge is the reason for its use in this cabinet design. The other reason is one of cost: Although it can be more expensive than a traditional hinge, you only require two or three types. Since the hinges are hidden, style is not a major consideration, so the hinges don't have to match the handles chosen by our clients.

This is a simple design to build, with advantages that many North American cabinetmakers have adopted for their cabinet design.

Hybrid Cabinet Design

As I mentioned briefly earlier, this cabinet design is a modular blend of European and North American cabinet construction methods. The final product, once installed, looks more traditional because of the use of the face frame on the cabinet. The main difference between the two styles, traditional and European, is the use of the face frame.

Figure 10-7
The European hidden hinge is adjustable in three directions.

Cabinet Types

I will refer to both standard and special cabinets, but don't let the terms confuse you. Each will be fully detailed. The standard cabinet design is the basis of the system and the special cabinets are modifications of the standard design to fit particular needs.

The carcass or body of the standard cabinets, both uppers and bases, is built with $\frac{5}{8}$ in. plastic laminated particle core board (PCB). Both upper and lower cabinets use full $\frac{5}{8}$ in. laminated PCB for strength and rigidity. The back panel is a full $\frac{5}{8}$ in. thick particle core board. This PCB back feature alone results in a cabinet that is of higher quality than most on the market today. Base and upper backing allows easier installation and a tighter cabinet, and eliminates the need to paint the walls inside and behind the cabinets. It also makes each cabinet a strong, free-standing, high-quality component.

Modifications or special cabinet carcass material can be substituted when the need arises. These include using $^{11}/_{16}$ in. wood veneer-covered PCB for microwave, pantry, or glass door cabinets, as well as other special applications. In a recent kitchen I completed, the architect specified $^{3}/_{4}$ in. white laminated particle core board as the carcass material. This specification was easily met with only a minor width increase in the cabinet back piece to accommodate the thicker carcass material. This cabinet design is so flexible that almost all special applications can be addressed with only minor changes.

Face-frame Cabinetry

Face-frame material for the standard cabinet is hardwood, usually oak, cherry or maple. The stiles, or vertical members of the face frame, are $^{3}/_{4}$ in. thick by 1 in. wide and $31^{3}/_{4}$ in. long. The rails, or horizontal pieces of the face frame, are $^{3}/_{4}$ in. thick by $1^{1}/_{2}$ in. wide and 2 in. shorter than the overall width in the standard cabinet design. Another way to express rail width is that rails are $^{1}/_{16}$ in. shorter than the inside cabinet dimension. This applies to both the upper and base cabinet face frames.

The standard upper and base cabinets that are referred to in the table, on the next page, to show the door width relationship, are full-door cabinets. Cabinet door height is variable, particularly in the base units, as overall door height depends upon whether or not a drawer assembly will be fitted above the door(s). Special size cabinets, such as those used over the stove, refrigerator, and sink, need smaller doors to match the reduced cabinet height. However, these doors are stock items with most door manufacturers because the sizes are industry standards.

Cabinet Doors

Doors used in this design, on the uppers or on base units without a drawer over the door, are $30^{1}/_{2}$ in. high. In the drawer section of this manual, I will describe the door height requirements when installing drawer, flip-out assemblies, or false drawer-fronts in the base units. Reduced-height cabinets, such as those previously mentioned, will also be detailed under separate headings.

These standard cabinet sizes are consistent with the door sizes produced by most manufacturers, both in height and width. Maintaining the basic cabinet sizes, wherever possible, allows us to use stock doors, which helps in producing a high quality cabinet for a reasonable price. The following table illustrates the uniformity of the design in that the same height door size is used in both the standard full door(s) upper and base cabinets.

Standard cabinet widths for both uppers and bases are in three-inch increments. The cabinet widths are as follows:

STANDARD CABINET SIZES

CABINET SIZE & TYPE	DOOR WIDTH	NUMBER OF DOORS
12 in. Upper or Base	11$\frac{1}{2}$ in.	1
15 in. Upper or Base	14$\frac{1}{2}$ in.	1
18 in. Upper or Base	17$\frac{1}{2}$ in.	1
21 in. Upper or Base	10$\frac{1}{2}$ in.	2
24 in. Upper or Base	11$\frac{1}{2}$ in.	2
27 in. Upper or Base	13 in.	2
30 in. Upper or Base	14$\frac{1}{2}$ in.	2
33 in. Upper or Base	16 in.	2
36 in. Upper or Base	17$\frac{1}{2}$ in.	2
24 in. Upper Corner	14$\frac{1}{2}$ in.	1
36 in. Corner Base	10 in.	2

CONSTRUCTION OVERVIEW

These cabinets have been designed without a center stile. When both doors of a two-door cabinet are open, you have complete access to the interior. This is made possible by the use of the fully adjustable European hinge. Each of the doors can be adjusted so that there is a $\frac{1}{16}$ in. gap between them when closed. European hinges are installed by way of 35mm holes drilled on the inside of each door. The hinges are of high quality and are simple to install. The other advantage of the European hinge is that they are hidden when the doors are closed, so you don't have to carry different styles of hinges. In most applications I use a 100- to 120-degree full-overlay cabinet hinge.

The gable ends (or sides) of the standard upper and base cabinets are the same length, 31 in. long. Only the depths are different: 10$\frac{5}{8}$ in. deep for the uppers and 22$\frac{1}{8}$ in. deep for the base units. These dimensions allow for maximum use of a standard 4x8 sheet of laminate-coated particle core board for carcass construction. The board length of 96 in. gives us three gable ends (three times 31 in. equals 93 in.). The gable depths of the standard cabinet allows for four upper gable ends and two base gable ends across the 48 in. width of the sheet. The interior depth of the standard uppers is 10$\frac{5}{8}$ in. plus the face-frame thickness of $\frac{3}{4}$ in. for a total interior depth of 11$\frac{3}{8}$ in. The interior base depth is 22$\frac{7}{8}$ in.

Five pieces of laminate PCB are needed for the uppers, two gable end units, one top, one bottom, and the backboard. However, the base units require only four pieces, two gable ends, one bottom, and one back. No top is required on the base as it is covered by the countertop assembly.

Base-cabinet Legs

Base units differ from uppers because they are fitted with European cabinet legs. These legs are independently adjustable, eliminate the need for

Benefits of Using the European Adjustable Leg System

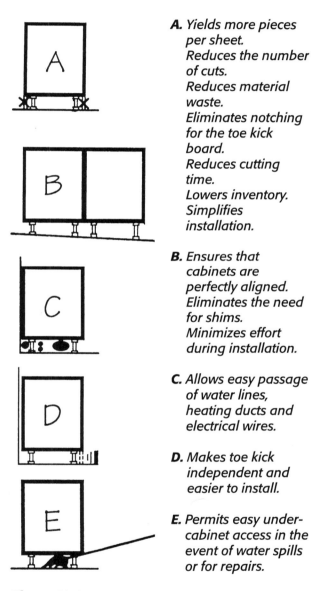

A. *Yields more pieces per sheet.*
Reduces the number of cuts.
Reduces material waste.
Eliminates notching for the toe kick board.
Reduces cutting time.
Lowers inventory.
Simplifies installation.

B. *Ensures that cabinets are perfectly aligned.*
Eliminates the need for shims.
Minimizes effort during installation.

C. *Allows easy passage of water lines, heating ducts and electrical wires.*

D. *Makes toe kick independent and easier to install.*

E. *Permits easy under-cabinet access in the event of water spills or for repairs.*

Figure 10-8
The Euro adjustable leg replaces the traditional cabinet base frame. Once you use this European cabinet leg system, you'll never want to return to the traditional methods of longer gable ends and 2x4 cabinet base support frames, which are difficult to level and shim during installation.

a cabinet kick-plate base assembly, and allow for a solid piece of 1in. by 4 in. hardwood board to be clipped on as the toe-kick board. The leg feature makes cabinet installation simple and accurate. Adjustable cabinet legs permit use of the 31 in. cabinet gables, which maximizes the yield from a standard sheet 4x8 sheet of PCB board.

Cabinet-interior Design

Maximum function and use of the cabinet interior was also important during my research into the cabinetry system. Most systems on the market have adjustable shelving as a standard design feature. The base units have adjustable shelving and pull-outs on European drawer slides. Both the upper corner cabinet and base corner cabinets use the Lazy Susan system. These design decisions offered the most flexibility, were functional and efficient to incorporate into the design from a production standpoint.

Figure 10-9
Upper cabinet interior showing the adjustable shelf system.

Figure 10-10
The upper corner cabinet showing an 18 in. round Lazy Susan assembly.

Figure 10-11
The 36 in. corner base with a 32 in. pie-cut Lazy Susan installed.

The upper cabinets in this system use the adjustable shelf as a standard. It provides an efficient and flexible cabinet which is accepted well by clients. I usually install two adjustable shelves in each standard cabinet, with a two-inch position adjustment.

The upper corner cabinet is almost always fitted with an 18 in. full-round two-shelf Lazy Susan as shown in Figure 10-10.

Base cabinets are constructed with one adjustable shelf, or one and possibly two pull-out drawer assemblies, depending on client needs. The corner base is usually fitted with a 32 in. pie-cut, two-shelf Lazy Susan assembly, shown in Figure 10-11.

Shelving is made of the same $5/8$ in. laminate-coated particle core board as the cabinets. The front or exposed edge of the PCB is covered with a plastic edging called cap molding. I usually construct full-depth base shelves to maximize the storage space in the cabinet. If the shelving is more than 30 in. wide, I often install a 1 in. by 2 in. hardwood cleat, running the full width of the shelf, on the rear underside of the shelf board, for added rigidity. Shelves can be loaded quite heavily, and I want the longer shelves strong so that they won't sag or break under heavy loads.

PCB QUALITY

The basic design is based on construction of a strong carcass or box as the body for each modular cabinet. The $5/8$ in. particle core board is butt-jointed and secured with special 2 in. PCB screws every four inches.

PCB quality is critical because the wood face frame is attached to the carcass-front using glue and 2 in. spiral finishing nails. Nails are driven through the face frame, countersunk, and the holes are covered with colored wood-filler wax, making them almost invisible. The cabinet door, when closed, covers the filled holes.

The plastic-laminate coated particle core board is the heart of the system and must be of the highest quality to produce quality butt-joints. Bargain-priced PCB will only lead to serious problems. There are many grades of PCB on the market, and some are simply not suitable for good quality carcass construction. I use an industrial grade, or cabinet grade by certain manufactures. Ratings and brand names may differ, but investigate the supply in your area and buy the highest grade available. It will prove to be cheaper in the long run.

Visual clues that might be useful when making your choice are the density, size and compactness of the wood chip in the board. The denser and finer the chips in the boards, and the more tightly compacted they appear to be, the higher the quality of the board. However, take some time to compare the specifications of the different material available in your area. Study the material, ask questions, and become well informed.

Working with PCB

Failure to drill a pilot hole prior to screw installation may cause joint failure. The low root (thin shaft), coarse-threaded PCB screws are specifically designed to thread into a $1/8$ in. hole for maximum hold. Without the hole, the screw can split

the PCB material. I suggest you use carbide-tipped saw blades and countersink drills when working with the high glue-content particle core board material.

Figure 10-12
Attaching the wood face frame to the cabinet carcass.

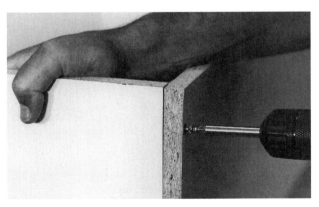

Figure 10-13
Proper assembly of the butt-jointed particle core boards for the carcass or box, and the wood stiles and rails for the face frames, is important. Two-inch screws designed for particle core boards must be used for the joints. These are best placed on 4 in. centers. It is also necessary to drill a $1/8$ in. countersunk pilot hole in the middle of the thickness of the board.

The quality of the cabinet depends upon a strong, square, accurately-built carcass. There are a few differences between upper and base cabinet design and assembly methods, but the basic principles of solid joints and square cabinets are common to all styles.

All of the 20 standard cabinets in this design are easy to assemble and are high-quality cabinets. Most of the cabinets I install are standard units. They can be built quickly and efficiently using good workshop procedures.

THE SHELF-HOLE JIG

A simple jig for drilling the shelf holes can be made with a piece of flat steel and plywood. The drawing in Figure 10-15 details the construction dimensions.

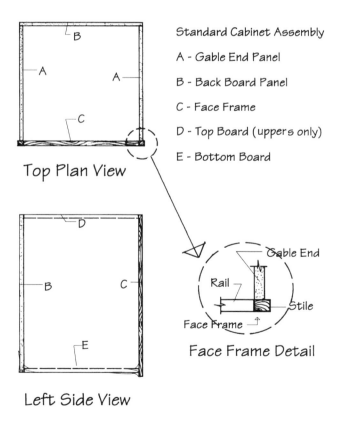

Standard Cabinet Assembly

A - Gable End Panel

B - Back Board Panel

C - Face Frame

D - Top Board (uppers only)

E - Bottom Board

Top Plan View

Face Frame Detail

Left Side View

Figure 10-14
Standard face-frame cabinet construction details.

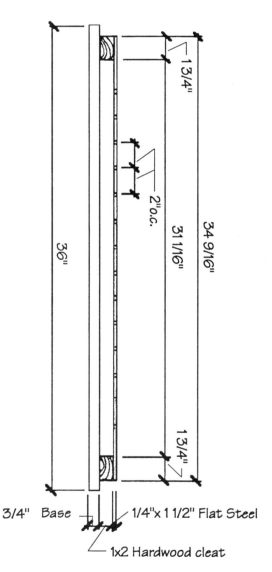

Figure 10-15
Build this simple hole jig so that all shelf holes are in alignment with each other. Standard gable ends slide under the flat steel, and the guide holes in the steel bar position the drill properly every time.

CHAPTER 11

UPPER FACE-FRAME CABINETS

In this section, I'll deal with the standard upper cabinet assembly. There are special cabinets and cabinet construction details that I will address in later chapters. However, understanding the basic principles of standard cabinet assembly, both bases and uppers, is the key to this system.

The table details size of face frame for each standard cabinet; all face frames are $\frac{3}{4}$ in. thick solid wood. The table applies to both uppers and bases.

Figure 11-1
The traditional style upper face-frame cabinet.

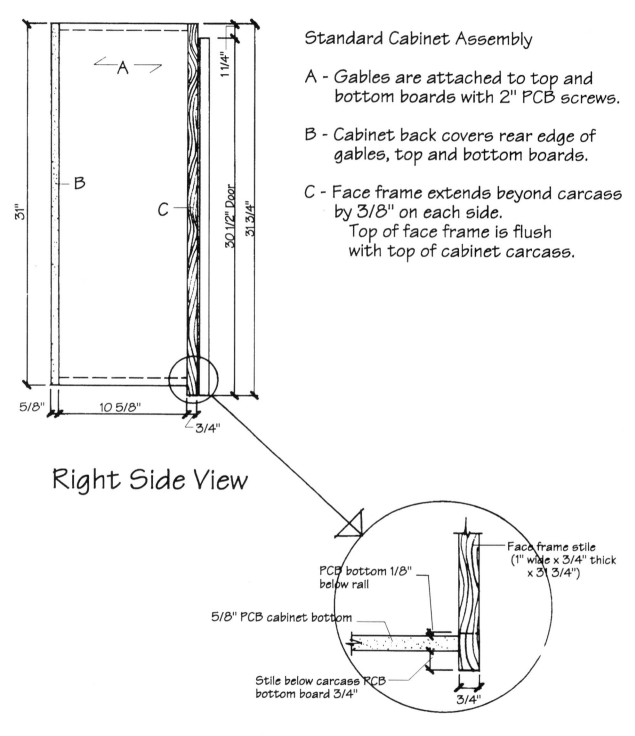

Right Side View

Standard Cabinet Assembly

A - Gables are attached to top and bottom boards with 2" PCB screws.

B - Cabinet back covers rear edge of gables, top and bottom boards.

C - Face frame extends beyond carcass by 3/8" on each side.
   Top of face frame is flush with top of cabinet carcass.

Face frame stile
(1" wide x 3/4" thick
x 31 3/4")

PCB bottom 1/8" below rail

5/8" PCB cabinet bottom

Stile below carcass PCB bottom board 3/4"

Corner Detail

Figure 11-2
Standard upper cabinet dimensions.

Face Frames for Upper Cabinets

CABINET WIDTH	TWO STILES WIDTH x HEIGHT	TWO RAILS HEIGHT x LENGTH
12 in.	1 in. x 31¾ in.	1½ in. x 10 in.
15 in.	1 in. x 31¾ in.	1½ in. x 13 in.
18 in.	1 in. x 31¾ in.	1½ in. x 16 in.
21 in.	1 in. x 31¾ in.	1½ in. x 19 in.
24 in.	1 in. x 31¾ in.	1½ in. x 22 in.
27 in.	1 in. x 31¾ in.	1½ in. x 25 in.
30 in.	1 in. x 31¾ in.	1½ in. x 28 in.
33 in.	1 in. x 31¾ in.	1½ in. x 31 in.
36 in.	1 in. x 31¾ in.	1½ in. x 34 in.

Face frames are constructed out of solid wood. For standard cabinets, stiles (vertical members) are ¾ in. thick by 1 in. wide by 31¾ in. long. The standard rails (horizontal members) are ¾ in. thick by 1½ in. high by 1/16 in. less than the interior width of the cabinet. For example, a 30 in. standard upper cabinet would require a face frame with two ¾ in. by 1 in. by 31¾ in. stiles

Tip: USE PBS SCREWS

Use 2-inch particle core board screws for the face-frame butt joints. You don't need to increase your hardware inventory because the PBS screw will work on both carcass joints and face frames. Countersunk pre-drilled holes should be made prior to screw insertion. This creates a tight joint and allows for a ³/₈ in. wood filler plug to be placed in the screw hole if this cabinet is an end cabinet that requires hidden screw holes.

and two ¾ in. by 1½ in. by 28 in. rails. The stiles are glued and screwed to the rails, resulting in a face frame for the 30 in. cabinet with an outside dimension of 30 in. wide by 31¾ in. high.

The completed face frames are secured to the cabinet carcass, flush with the top of the cabinet, and extend ¾ in. below the bottom of the cabinet. I secure the face frames to the carcass with glue and 2 in. spiral finishing nails at 8 in. centers.

The corner butt joints for the face frames should be glued and secured with two 2 in. wood screws at each corner.

Standard upper cabinet size and construction practices will be addressed first. The table is a cut list with all the carcass component sizes based on ⅝ in. laminate-coated particle core board material. I usually use the white plastic-laminated material because of its ready availability and the clean

Standard Upper Cabinet Cut List

UPPER CABINET	TWO GABLES	TOP & BOTTOM	ONE BACK
12 in. wide	$10^5/8$ in. x 31 in.	$10^5/8$ in. x $10^1/16$ in.	$11^1/2$ in. x 31 in.
15 in. wide	$10^5/8$ in. x 31 in.	$10^5/8$ in. x $13^1/16$ in.	$14^1/2$ in. x 31 in.
18 in. wide	$10^5/8$ in. x 31 in.	$10^5/8$ in. x $16^1/16$ in.	$17^1/2$ in. x 31 in.
21 in. wide	$10^5/8$ in. x 31 in.	$10^5/8$ in. x $19^1/16$ in.	$20^1/2$ in. x 31 in.
24 in. wide	$10^5/8$ in. x 31 in.	$10^5/8$ in. x $22^1/16$ in.	$23^1/2$ in. x 31 in.
27 in. wide	$10^5/8$ in. x 31 in.	$10^5/8$ in. x $25^1/16$ in.	$26^1/2$ in. x 31 in.
30 in. wide	$10^5/8$ in. x 31 in.	$10^5/8$ in. x $28^1/16$ in.	$29^1/2$ in. x 31 in.
33 in. wide	$10^5/8$ in. x 31 in.	$10^5/8$ in. x $31^1/16$ in.	$32^1/2$ in. x 31 in.
36 in. wide	$10^5/8$ in. x 31 in.	$10^5/8$ in. x $34^1/16$ in.	$35^1/2$ in. x 31 in.

look it gives to the cabinet interior. White accessories such as towel racks, drawer slides and Lazy Susan assemblies are also readily available from most suppliers as stock items.

In addition to the pieces for each upper carcass assembly, you will require a minimum of two shelf pieces for each cabinet. The shelves for the upper cabinets are always $10^5/8$ in. deep and $1/16$ in. less, in total width, than the top or bottom carcass boards. For example, in the case of a 30 in. wide standard upper, I would need two shelf boards, each $10^5/8$ in. deep by 28 in. wide.

Some of the dimensions, such as the top and bottom carcass boards, are as close as $1/16$ in. because I calculate them to ensure that the interior dimension of the cabinet is just slightly wider than the inside dimension of the cabinet face frame. This guarantees that the face frame will completely cover the exposed edges of the PCB carcass.

The back is slightly wider than required for another reason. Take the 30in. cabinet as an example: Add the bottom board width of $28^1/16$ in. to the combined thickness of both gable ends (twice $5/8$ in. equals $1^1/4$ in.), for a total of $29^5/16$ in. The backboard dimension in the chart for the 30 in.

Tip: DRILL PILOT HOLE

To avoid splitting and to ensure a solid joint, always drill a pilot hole before installing a screw or a nail into particle core board. I've tried to use my finishing air-nailer for securing the face frames, but without much success. Nail deflection, because of the high glue content of the particle core board, can happen and the nail may break through the finished side of the gable end board. Countersink the nails and use a wax stick matching the finished color of the cabinet wood to hide the holes.

cabinet is $29\frac{1}{2}$ in., which is obviously too wide. However, some PCB material is actually a metric equivalent of $\frac{5}{8}$ in. and slightly thicker, while some material of different production runs vary slightly in thickness. For this reason the backboard is cut a little wide, then I can trim it flush with a router after installation on the carcass.

Complete coverage of the carcass edges on the back of the cabinet is important. This $\frac{5}{8}$ in. backboard adds strength and stability to the cabinets. The backboard, secured to the carcass edges with 2 in. particle board screws at 4 in. centers, creates a free-standing, extremely strong modular unit. The cabinets are secured to the wall by screwing through this backboard and, since the backboard fully covers the carcass, screws can be placed in any location on the board. The upper cabinets are actually hung by screwing through the backboard and into the wall studs, while the base cabinet is anchored to the wall to stabilize the cabinet position only, since most of the base cabinet weight is taken on the adjustable legs

Clients see this backboard as a plus because the interior of this cabinet is virtually maintenance-free and the wall behind the cabinet does not need painting. While these features are important to the client, the major advantages for the cabinetmaker are the structural stability and the ease of installation.

STANDARD UPPER CABINET ASSEMBLY

In the case of upper cabinets, first ensure that all PCB and face-frame components are accurately cut to size. Follow the assembly steps as detailed below:

1. Drill the holes in each gable for the adjustable shelves, if the cabinet is to be so equipped. During assembly, ensure that the top-to-top relationship of each gable end is maintained, particularly if the holes are started at different distances from the top and bottom of the gable end. I've made that mistake once or twice, and it's embarrassing to discover after you've finished assembly of the carcass (Fig. 11-3).

Figure 11-3
Drill the adjustable shelf holes in each gable end.

Tip: TRIM BACKBOARD
After installing the backboard, trim it with a flush-trim router bit equipped with a pilot bearing. But be careful: PCB is tough on router bits and the router can kick back. Hold the cabinet and the router tightly, but keep your hand away from the back of the router.

2. Fasten one gable end to the edge of the bottom board, making sure the joint is square and flush. Drill a ⅛ in. countersink pilot hole for each of the three 2 in. PCB screws. Do not over-tighten or apply so much force to the screws that they strip their threaded hole. Take care to drill the pilot hole so that it's in the center of the edge on the board to which you are fastening the gable end, in this case the bottom board of the carcass. Mark a line ⁵⁄₁₆ in. up from the gable end edge with a marking gauge as a guide for your pilot hole. This will guarantee maximum hold for the screw and will result in a very strong joint. Connect the remaining three corner joints in the same manner (Fig. 11-4).

3. For verification at this point, referring to a 30 in. upper cabinet as an example, you should have a four-sided frame with inside dimensions of 28¹⁄₁₆ in. wide (the width of the bottom and top carcass boards) by 29¾ in. high (the length of the gable end minus the thickness of the top and bottom carcass boards) (Fig. 11-5).

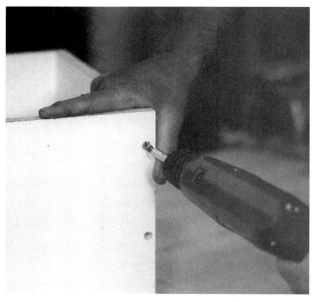

Figure 11-4
Attach gable ends to the top and bottom boards.

Figure 11-5
Verify dimensions as you assemble the cabinet.

Figure 11-6
Attach the cabinet backboard using 2 in. screws at 4 in. centers.

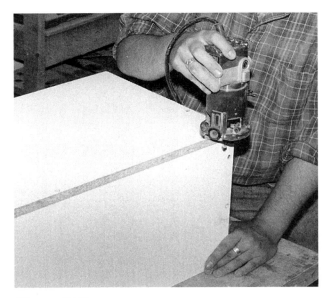

Figure 11-7
Flush trim the backboard with a router.

4. Attach the backboard to the carcass box flush with three edges of the backboard. This will square the carcass. Because the backboards are intentionally cut wider to accommodate thickness variances in the PCB material, you will have one side with a slight overhang. Secure the back to the carcass frame using 2 in. PCB screws at 4 in. centers. Use a marking gauge to draw lines $\frac{5}{16}$ in. in from the edges as a guide for the pilot holes. One side of the back has a slight overhang, so take this into account when marking guide lines on that side (Fig. 11-6).

5. After securing the back, flush trim the overhang with a flush-trim bit in a router. This joint will not be seen, so I use an old carbide router bit because the PCB material dulls cutting tools (Fig. 11-7).

6. At this point, ensure that the holes for the adjustable shelf pins are in correct side-to-side relationship with each other and that the carcass is square. Either measure the diagonals of the carcass and verify that they are equal, or use a framing square on the inside of the carcass.

Assemble the face frame as described earlier. Referring again to a 30 in. upper cabinet, verify that the outside measurement of the face frame is 30 in. wide by $31\frac{3}{4}$ in. long. The stiles should be 1 in. wide and the rails should be $1\frac{1}{2}$ in. high (Fig. 11-8).

Figure 11-8
Face frame assembly detail.

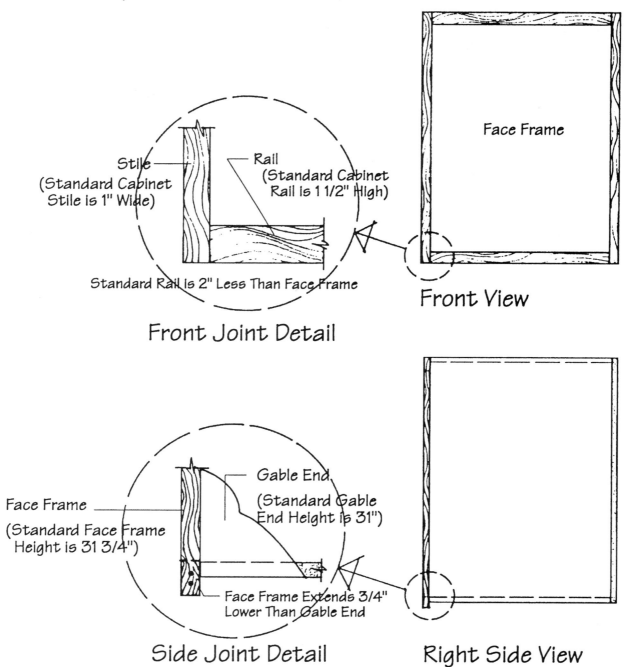

Stile
(Standard Cabinet
Stile is 1" Wide)

Rail
(Standard Cabinet
Rail is 1 1/2" High)

Face Frame

Standard Rail Is 2" Less Than Face Frame

Front Joint Detail

Front View

Face Frame
(Standard Face Frame
Height is 31 3/4")

Gable End
(Standard Gable
End Height is 31")

Face Frame Extends 3/4"
Lower Than Gable End

Side Joint Detail

Right Side View

Figure 11-9
Install the face frame on the carcass using glue and 2 in. spiral nails.

Figure 11-10
Set the nails and fill holes with a wax stick or putty to match final cabinet color.

7. Apply glue to the four carcass edges and place the outside face-frame top edge flush with the outside top edge of the carcass. The face frame should fully cover the carcass edges. The inside dimension of the face frame should be slightly smaller than the inside dimension of the carcass. The carcass bottom and top are cut $\frac{1}{16}$ in. larger than the face-frame rails to guarantee full carcass-edge coverage by the face frame. Divide the difference between the two inside edges. Secure the top corner of the face frame to the carcass body using 2 in. spiral finish nails in a pilot hole slightly smaller than the nail thickness.

Drill the pilot hole so that it centers, as much as possible, on the PCB edge. Secure the other top corner so that the top outside of the face frame is flush with the top outside edge of the carcass. Secure the bottom two corners, making sure that the slight overhang of the face frame inside the carcass is maintained equally on both sides.

Install the remaining nails at 8 in. centers, maintaining the overhang (Fig. 11-9).

8. The bottom rail should hang below the cabinet carcass by $\frac{3}{4}$ in. and the face frame sides should extend $\frac{3}{8}$ in. beyond each side of the carcass.

9. Set the nails below the surface and fill the holes with a wax stick that will match the finished color of the cabinet wood. Doors and shelves can be installed now, though I will detail door installation techniques later (Fig. 11-10).

Tip: USE PUTTY PENCIL
I use a light oak-colored putty pencil to fill nail holes for clear oil-based polyurethane-finished oak. Use a plumber's torch to heat the putty, and wipe the excess off with a rag before it cools. The hole is almost invisible after finishing.

BUILDING UPPER CORNER CABINETS

The following is a cut list for the standard 24 in. upper corner cabinet with an 18 in. round two-shelf Lazy Susan unit. It's one cabinet that you'll build for a great many kitchens.

Cutting components to their proper size is important. Cut the top and bottom boards to the size stated in the above table, leaving the angle

DESCRIPTION	QUANTITY	SIZE	COMMENTS
GABLE END	2	10⅝ in. x 31 in.	
TOP & BOTTOM	1 EACH	22⅛ in. x 22⅛ in.	Cut as illustrated in Figure 11-11
BACK	1	22¾ in. x 31 in.	
BACK	1	23⅜ in. x 31 in.	

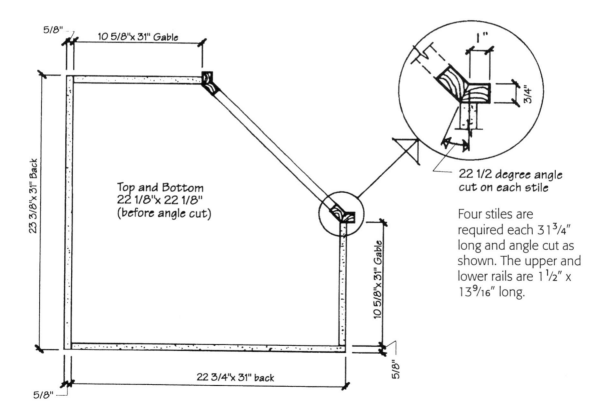

Figure 11-11
Upper corner cabinet construction diagram.

cut until you are ready to assemble the pieces.

As illustrated, pay particular attention to the cut sizes of the backboards. One back is $^5/_8$ in. wider, to allow for the required overlaps in the boards during assembly.

The standard 24 in. upper corner cabinet is popular with many clients. I have installed at least one in almost every kitchen I have built. It is, however, somewhat difficult to build, but is not beyond the scope of most cabinetmakers. The following are steps for proper assembly. Please refer to Figure 11-11.

1. There are six boards required for this cabinet, cut as indicated in the cut size table.

2. This cabinet is almost always fitted with a two-shelf 18in. Lazy Susan assembly and therefore holes for adjustable shelves are not required.

3. Assemble the boards as shown in Figure 11-11, and ensure all joints are square and secure. Drill $^1/_8$ in. countersink pilot holes and use 2 in. PCB screws at 4 in. centers.

4. Cut the six wood parts for the face-frame assembly and assemble as indicated. This face frame can be a little difficult to assemble, however, the use of angle clamps will aid in holding the stiles in place while they are glued and screwed to each other. Cut the parts as close as possible to the indicated angle and assemble with care.

5. Glue and nail the face frame to the carcass in the same manner as the other cabinets. Install the

face frame so that the outside top of it is flush with the outside top of the corner carcass (Fig. 11-12)

6. The inside surface of the stiles are not flush with the gable ends, as in the other cabinets, so a face frame hinge plate is used to secure the hinges and door for this cabinet.

Figure 11-12
Install the face frame on the upper corner carcass with glue and 2 in. spiral nails.

CHAPTER 12

FACE-FRAME BASE CABINETS

Most of what you will build will be standard base cabinets, so a systematic approach is very helpful to have. The table atop the next page gives the sizes (cut list) for the PCB pieces required to assemble standard base cabinets.

Figure 12-1
Traditional style face-frame base cabinets.

Face Frame Base Cabinets

BASE CABINET	TWO GABLES	ONE BOTTOM	ONE BACK
12 in. wide	$22^{1}/_{8}$ in. x 31 in.	$22^{1}/_{8}$ in. x $10^{1}/_{16}$ in.	$11^{1}/_{2}$ in. x 31 in.
15 in. wide	$22^{1}/_{8}$ in. x 31 in.	$22^{1}/_{8}$ in. x $13^{1}/_{16}$ in.	$14^{1}/_{2}$ in. x 31 in.
18 in. wide	$22^{1}/_{8}$ in. x 31 in.	$22^{1}/_{8}$ in. x $16^{1}/_{16}$ in.	$17^{1}/_{2}$ in. x 31 in.
21 in. wide	$22^{1}/_{8}$ in. x 31 in.	$22^{1}/_{8}$ in. x $19^{1}/_{16}$ in.	$20^{1}/_{2}$ in. x 31 in.
24 in. wide	$22^{1}/_{8}$ in. x 31 in.	$22^{1}/_{8}$ in. x $22^{1}/_{16}$ in.	$23^{1}/_{2}$ in. x 31 in.
27 in. wide	$22^{1}/_{8}$ in. x 31 in.	$22^{1}/_{8}$ in. x $25^{1}/_{16}$ in.	$26^{1}/_{2}$ in. x 31 in.
30 in. wide	$22^{1}/_{8}$ in. x 31 in.	$22^{1}/_{8}$ in. x $28^{1}/_{16}$ in.	$29^{1}/_{2}$ in. x 31 in.
33 in. wide	$22^{1}/_{8}$ in. x 31 in.	$22^{1}/_{8}$ in. x $31^{1}/_{16}$ in.	$32^{1}/_{2}$ in. x 31 in.
36 in. wide	$22^{1}/_{8}$ in. x 31 in.	$22^{1}/_{8}$ in. x $34^{1}/_{16}$ in.	$35^{1}/_{2}$ in. x 31 in.

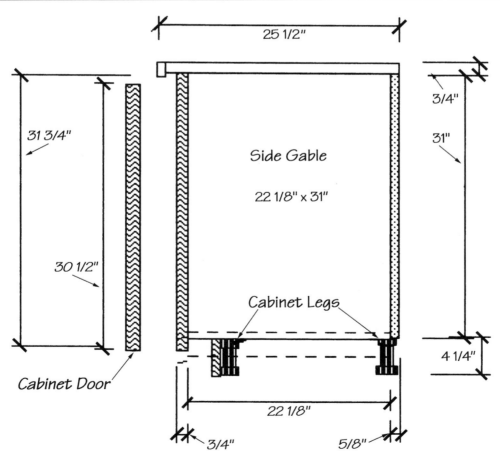

Figure 12-2
The standard face-frame cabinet base dimensions.

Refer to Figure 12-2 for assembly position details and the face-frame position on the cabinet. It may be necessary to cut shelves for the base units, if your design requires shelves instead of pull-outs. Shelves for the base unit are 22 $^1/_8$ in. deep and $^1/_{16}$ in. less than the width of the base bottom.

The $^1/_{16}$ in. added-width measurement of the bottom is to ensure that the inside dimension of the cabinet is just slightly larger than the inside dimension of the face frame, so that the carcass edges will be fully covered by the face frame. With standard base cabinets, a top board is not required as the countertop will cover this area.

NOTE: Before cutting the PCB material, be sure to verify that it is indeed $^5/_8$ in. thick. I have seen variances in this product, even from the same manufacturer, that could cause you some trouble. Take the variances, if any, into account when creating your cut list.

BUILDING BASE CABINETS

Base cabinet assembly uses the same basic procedures as upper cabinets. However, there are a few minor differences which I will detail in the following steps. Please refer once again to Figure 12-2 as a guide.

1. Drill holes in each gable end for the adjustable shelf pins, if the cabinet is to be so equipped. If adjustable shelves are to be installed, ensure that

Tip: SHELF PIN JIG
The same shelf-hole jig is used to drill top as well as bottom gables for adjustable shelf pins.

the top-to-top relationship of the gable ends is maintained properly.

2. Install the adjustable legs on the cabinet base board, using the screws and installation techniques suggested by the manufacturer of the legs you are using. Generally, the legs are attached by means of holes drilled through the base board. The screw is then threaded into the leg with the base board sandwiched between the screw and the leg. Set the legs 3$^1/_2$ in. back from the front edge of the baseboard to allow setback for the toe-kick space. Drill the holes in such a way that when the leg is installed it will extend beyond the back and both side edges by $^5/_8$ in. This will allow the gable ends and backboard to rest on the leg flanges, providing additional support for the cabinet. Part of the load placed on the cabinet will then be transferred through the legs to the floor.

Figure 12-3
Install adjustable cabinet legs on the base board.

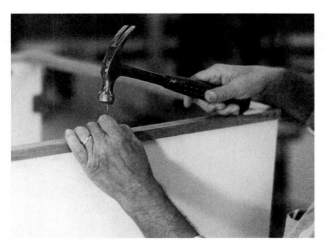

Figure 12-4
Installing the base cabinet face-frame.

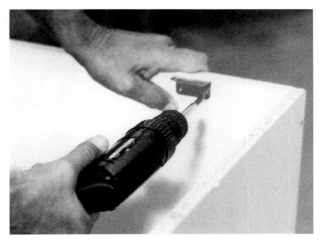

Figure 12-5
Attach countertop clips with ⁵⁄₈ in. screws.

3. Fasten the gable ends and back to the base board as in the upper cabinet assembly instructions.

4. Install the face frame in the same manner as detailed in the upper cabinet assembly instructions. The difference in this step is that the base carcass does not have a top board, therefore the gable end tops can move easily. Make sure the top edge of the face frame is flush with the top corner edge of the gable end, and that the inside edge of the face frame is slightly past the inside edge of the gable end. Secure that corner with glue and a nail, then secure the other top corner. Fasten the bottom corners, maintaining the inside face frame overhang (approximately $1/32$ in.), then secure the face frame to the carcass with glue and 2in. finishing nails at 8 in. centers (Fig. 4).

5. The face frame should extend past the bottom of the carcass base board by $3/4$ in. and the face-frame sides should be $3/8$ in. past the outside of each gable end.

6. At this point, countertop clips (as shown in Figure 12-5) are installed flush with the top and back edges of the carcass. Two are required per side, spaced equally around the top perimeter. These are secured with $5/8$ in. screws and will be used to fasten the countertop in place.

7. Set the face-frame nails and fill the holes, trim the backboard overhang, and verify the cabinet is square.

The cabinet is now ready for doors, drawers and/or shelves.

Tip: MARK EDGE
Always mark the top edge of cabinet parts with a colored marker so that you can tell the top from the bottom at a glance. By doing this, you'll avoid flipping a gable end during assembly.

Figure 12-6
The 36 in. corner base cabinet with Lazy Susan assembly.

BUILDING BASE CORNER CABINETS

To build the corner base cabinet, refer to Figure 12-7 for assembly and angle-cutting details, as well as for the face frame cutting and assembly.

The 36 in. standard corner base cabinet is a popular and useful kitchen cabinet. In combination with an installed 32 in. pie-cut Lazy Susan assembly, this cabinet creates useful corner space that is otherwise wasted. The following steps describe the assembly process.

1. There are six PCB pieces as indicated in the cut list table. Cut the pieces accurately. Do not cut the angles on the 18 in. by 31 in. backboard at this time. I recommend that you cut it with straight cuts to the stated 18 in. by 31 in. size.

2. Install the cabinet legs in the positions indicated in the drawing. Maintain the 3½ in. setback from the front edges of the cabinet. Remember that this setback is required for toe-kick spacing on all the base cabinets. Position the other legs so that they will extend out from the edge of the

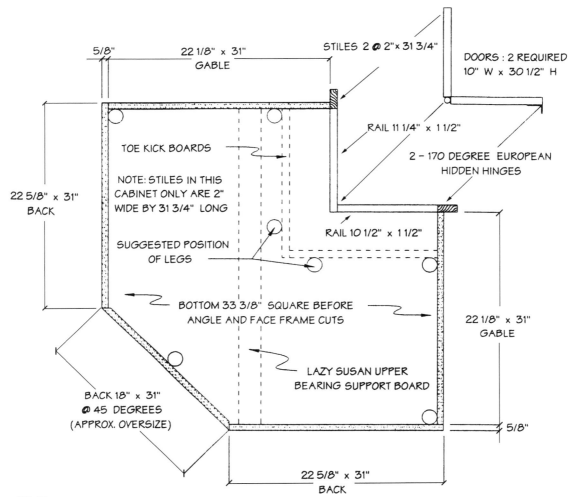

5/8"
22 1/8" x 31" GABLE
STILES 2 @ 2"x 31 3/4"
DOORS : 2 REQUIRED 10" W x 30 1/2" H
RAIL 11 1/4" x 1 1/2"
TOE KICK BOARDS
2 – 170 DEGREE EUROPEAN HIDDEN HINGES
22 5/8" x 31" BACK
NOTE: STILES IN THIS CABINET ONLY ARE 2" WIDE BY 31 3/4" LONG
RAIL 10 1/2" x 1 1/2"
SUGGESTED POSITION OF LEGS
BOTTOM 33 3/8" SQUARE BEFORE ANGLE AND FACE FRAME CUTS
22 1/8" x 31" GABLE
BACK 18" x 31" @ 45 DEGREES (APPROX. OVERSIZE)
LAZY SUSAN UPPER BEARING SUPPORT BOARD
5/8"
22 5/8" x 31" BACK

Figure 12-7
The 36 in. corner base construction diagram.

The standard 36 in. corner base unit is usually equipped with a 32 in. pie-cut two-shelf Lazy Susan assembly.

Corner Base Cabinet

DESCRIPTION	QUANTITY	SIZE	COMMENTS
GABLE END	2	22$\frac{1}{8}$ in. x 31 in.	
SIDE	2	22$\frac{5}{8}$ in. x 31 in.	
BACK	1	18 in. x 31in.	Angle cut as Illus. in Figure 12-7
BOTTOM	1	33$\frac{3}{8}$ in. x 33$\frac{3}{8}$ in.	Cut as Illus. in Figure 12-7

base board by $\frac{5}{8}$ in. to aid in supporting the cabinet gable ends. Assemble the cabinet boards as shown, leaving the 18in. by 31in. backboard until all others are secured.

Tip: DON'T TIGHTEN LEGS

When installing cabinet legs that will overhang the base board and support a gable end, don't fully tighten the leg. A tightened leg will not allow the gable end to come down far enough to be flush with the bottom edge of the base board. Secure the gable to base board then fully tighten the leg assembly.

3. Measure the opening for the backboard, and fit the back by cutting 45-degree angles on each side. The first time you build one of these cabinets, it may be helpful to angle-cut the backboard so that it's a little larger and trial-fit the back. Continue cutting the backboard slightly smaller after each trial fit until it's perfect.

4. Cut and assemble the face frame as indicated, with two stiles 2 in. wide by $31\frac{3}{4}$ in. long; and four rails, two of them $1\frac{1}{2}$ in. wide by $11\frac{1}{4}$ in. long and the other two $1\frac{1}{2}$ in. wide by $10\frac{1}{2}$ in. long. The $11\frac{1}{4}$ in. rails overlap the $10\frac{1}{2}$ in. rail ends, forming an equal dimension right-angled frame. Install the frame so that the inside faces of the gable ends are flush with the inside surfaces of the face-frame stiles.

5. Install the angle clips (two per gable end) so that the counter top can be secured.

6. This cabinet is now ready for the 32 in. pie-cut Lazy Susan and the doors.

PANTRY & MICROWAVE CABINETS

Pantry and microwave cabinets share the same basic carcass assembly. The gable ends are $80\frac{1}{2}$ in. high and as deep as you require. The top and bottom shelves follow the width rules for standard cabinets, and the back is $80\frac{1}{2}$ in. high by the total width of the bottom board, plus the two gable end thicknesses. There may be one or two additional fixed shelves, depending on the style of the cabinet. The face frame is $81\frac{1}{4}$ in. high with 1in. wide stiles and a $1\frac{1}{2}$ in. top and bottom rail. The face frame may also contain up to five additional rails, depending on the drawer and door combination. Each cabinet is usually fitted with adjustable shelves, drawers, pull-outs or a combination of all three.

Figure 12-8
Pantry cabinets are popular additions in many new kitchens.

Figure 12-9
Microwave cabinets are often added in kitchen renovation projects.

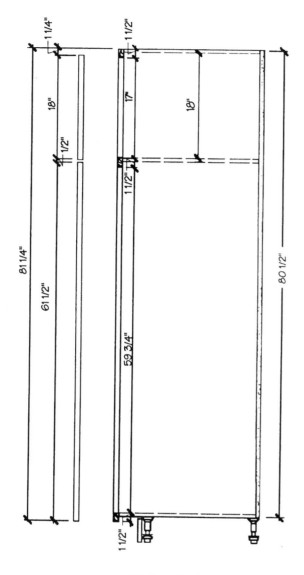

Right Side View

Figure 12-10
Typical pantry cabinet dimensions.

Figure 12-10 details the construction of a pantry cabinet in which I usually install adjustable shelves or pull-outs. The pantry cabinet is built using two doors with three European hinges installed for the lower, larger door(s). The lower, larger door is an industry standard $61\frac{1}{2}$ in. high and the upper door is 18in. high. A $\frac{1}{2}$ in. gap is left between the upper and lower doors, so that we maintain the $1\frac{1}{4}$ in. space at the top of the face frame. A rail is installed, with a fixed shelf board, at the point where the upper and lower doors meet. This cabinet is a popular addition in many kitchen renovation projects.

Microwave cabinets, as shown in Figure 12-11, follow all the standard cabinet rules and usually contain a lower drawer bank or pull-outs behind doors and adjustable shelves behind the upper doors. The middle opening usually contains the microwave. A standard cabinet width of 27 in., which has a 25 in. inside face frame width, is large enough for most microwave ovens. If you are going to build this cabinet as part of a renovation project, arrange for an electrician to install an outlet in the oven space.

To install four drawers in the base of this cabinet, follow the same rules and dimensions that apply to a four-drawer-bank base cabinet as explained in chapter 13. Remember to use spacing cleats, as shown in the next chapter, if installing pull-outs behind the doors on either cabinet. The upper sections of these cabinets are usually fitted with adjustable shelves.

The pantry and microwave cabinet carcasses are built using wood veneer-covered particle core board, since a good portion of the cabinets is visible. An $^{11}/_{16}$ in. wood veneer board will allow the face frame to extend $^{5}/_{16}$ in. beyond the carcass, which makes it easy to use wood door-stop molding around the visible perimeter. This technique covers screws and softens the look of these large cabinets.

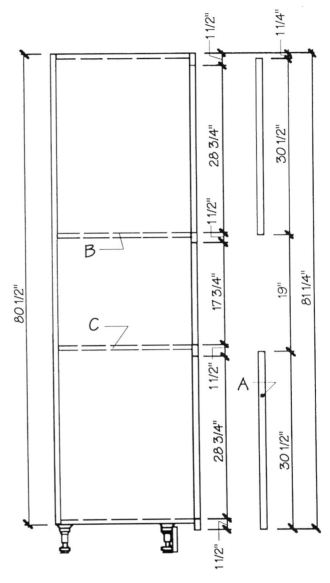

Left Side View

Figure 12-11
Microwave cabinet dimensions.
(A) Lower is fitted with 30^1/$_2$ in. high doors or four drawer unit.
(B) Fixed shelf
(C) Fixed shelf
Most cabinets are 27 in. wide to accept a normal width microwave unit.

CHAPTER 13

SPECIAL CABINETS AND ACCESSORIES

BUILDING A DRAWER-OVER-DOOR BASE

One popular base cabinet is the drawer-over-door unit shown in Figure 13-2. I usually install at least one of these units in each kitchen I build. The large drawer, particularly in a cabinet such as the 30 in. base unit, is a useful addition to most kitchens. This cabinet style is also used when a counter cooktop is installed. In that case, a false drawer front is permanently attached to hide the cooktop hardware when the doors are opened.

The interior of the cabinet, behind the doors, can be fitted with either a pull-out or an adjustable shelf. Determine the required interior cabinet accessories during the design phase, so that you can drill holes for the shelf or attach spacing cleats for the pull-out during the cabinet assembly stage.

Figure 13-1
Drawer-over-door base cabinet.

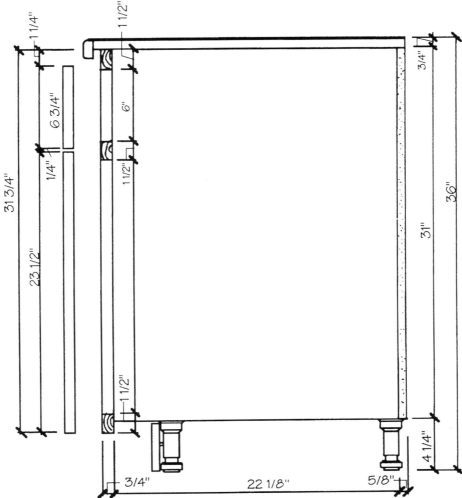

Figure 13-2
Drawer-over-door dimensions.

Construction procedures for this cabinet are identical to those for the standard base cabinet, except for an added rail piece to cover the space between the door and drawer. The general design rule that applies is to maintain the 30½ in. overall height so that we have 1¼ in. revealed at the top of the face frame. Our standard door height is 30½ in. for full-door cabinets. When we construct a drawer-over-door cabinet, or any other combination cabinet, we want to maintain the 30½ in. height so that all doors and drawers are at the same level.

Maintaining this uniform line is visually pleasing, especially with base cabinets. The combination of a 23½ in. door and a 6¾ in. high drawer-face, plus the ¼ in. space between them, gives us the required 30½ in. height.

Tip: MAINTAIN HEIGHT

Any combination of drawers and doors can be designed, as long as you maintain the total door, drawers, or door/drawer height of 30 1/2 in.

Drawer construction, described in detail later in this chapter, uses the ⅝ in. laminate-covered PCB box method, mounted on European drawer glides. Door installation is the same as with all other doors except that we are using a 23½ in. high industry-standard size door. If we use the 30 in. base cabinet as an example, we would require two doors 23½ in. high by 14½ in. wide. The drawer face would be 6¾ n. high by 29¹⁄₁₆ in. wide. The drawer face width is a combination of the widths of the two doors plus a gap allowance between the two doors of ¹⁄₁₆ in. I try to adjust the center gap on a two-door cabinet as tight as ¹⁄₁₆ in. However, this is not always practical if there are constant humidity changes in the client's house.

In most of my kitchen projects, drawer faces are made from solid 1in. by 8 in. hardwood. I decided on this method for a number of reasons, primarily, because 1in. by 8 in. lumber is dressed to ¾ in. by 7¼ in. so I don't have to be concerned with edge joining boards. This reduces the time and cost required to manufacture the cabinets, for me as well as for the client.

Cabinet door style will determine the amount of work needed to produce a compatible drawer face. In most cases, I use a router to apply a round-over or cove detail to the drawer edge. This will produce a good-looking drawer face for almost all applications.

There has been the odd occasion when the client has wanted a fancy and intricate drawer face. In those cases, I ordered special-size drawer faces from my door supplier. However, the cost per drawer assembly was adjusted from the standard price schedule and the difference was charged to the client.

FOUR-DRAWER BASE CABINETS

Almost every kitchen I've built has at least one of the four-drawer base cabinets shown in Figure 13-3. They are primarily used as a cutlery center and are often located near the sink and dishwasher.

Figure 13-3
A four-drawer base cabinet ready for installation.

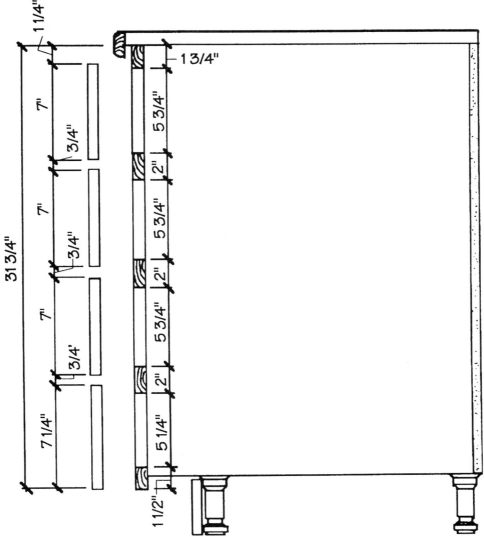

Figure 13-4
Construction diagram for the four-drawer base cabinet.

The four-drawer cabinet is nothing more than a standard base unit fitted with extra rails to hide the gaps between the drawers. As shown in Figure 13-4, there are some special spacing and rail size considerations so that the $30\frac{1}{2}$ in. overall door, drawer/door, or multiple drawer height is maintained.

Use the standard drawer-box construction method detailed later in this chapter and mount the drawer boxes on European drawer glides. I usually make all the drawer boxes the same height, using the minimum opening size as my guide.

The drawer glides that I use require that the drawer box be 1 in. shorter in height than the opening, so I construct all drawer boxes $4\frac{1}{4}$ in. high, to save cutting time. The drawer faces are 1 in. by 8 in. hardwood boards which are edge-routed to match the door style. Dressed or finished 1 in. by 8 in. material is actually $\frac{3}{4}$ in. by $7\frac{1}{4}$ in., so my maximum drawer-face height is $7\frac{1}{4}$ in., allowing me to use standard boards.

Carefully mount the drawer faces to the drawer box, in the positions shown in Figure 13-4, with four $1\frac{1}{4}$ in. wood screws on the inside of the drawer box, into the back of the drawer face.

Construct the face frame using the dimensions shown in Figure 13-4. There are a total of five rails which, when installed, will divide the face frame so that there are four drawer-openings. Rails are cut at the height shown and are 2 in. less in width than the outside face-frame dimension. Fasten each rail with glue and two 2 in. screws. If this cabinet is to be used as an open end-run cabinet, counterbore the screw holes so that they can be filled with wood plugs,

Tip: INSTALL CENTER SCREW

I find that one screw placed in the center allows me to install the drawer to check the alignment prior to fastening the four corner screws.

Tip: FILL ODD SPACES

We don't have to be concerned about industry-standard door sizes with this cabinet, so it can be any width. Use this cabinet to fill odd-size spaces in many situations.

Using a 30 in. four-drawer base cabinet as an example, and the standard $\frac{3}{4}$ in. thick wood, this face frame would require two stiles, each 1 in. wide by $31\frac{3}{4}$ in. long, three rails 2 in. wide by 28 in. long, one rail $1\frac{3}{4}$ in. wide by 28 in. long, and one rail $1\frac{1}{2}$ in. wide by 28 in. long.

Apply the basic system design rule: The inside face frame width should equal the inside carcass width. Then you can make this cabinet any size you require. For example, if I had to fill a $26\frac{5}{8}$ in. space, I would construct a face frame with 1 in. wide stiles and a rail width of $24\frac{5}{8}$ in. The carcass bottom board would be $24\frac{5}{8}$ in. wide, equal to the inside face frame width. Remember, you don't have to be concerned with standard door sizes because you can make the drawer faces any width as long as they are 1 in. shorter than the outside face frame width. All other carcass boards follow the standard rules, gable ends are 31 in. high by $22\frac{1}{8}$ in. wide and the backboard width is the total of the base board width plus the gable end thicknesses by 31 in. high.

END CABINETS

Base and upper cabinets that are at the end of a run and are open to view on one side must be finished so that we don't see the PCB gable ends. These open end-run cabinets should be identified in the planning stage, prior to cabinet construction. To allow for the finishing trim that is used on end-run cabinets, I increase the stile width by $\frac{1}{4}$ in. on the side to be finished.

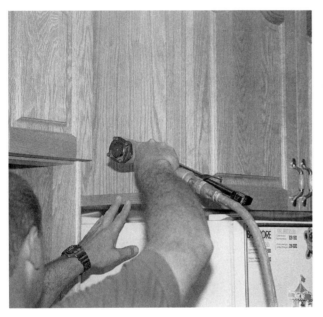

Figure 13-5
Open-ended cabinets are finished with a $\frac{1}{4}$ in. panel and molding.

Increasing the stile width on standard upper and base cabinets does not alter the dimensions of any other cabinet part. This stile-width increase technique is needed for end finishing, contour fitting of the cabinet to a wall, or custom cabinet fitting of a cabinet run that is closed by walls on both ends. In the planning stage, I usually designate a

cabinet that requires increased stile width with a measurement and side designation. A 30 in. cabinet that will be used as an open left end-run cabinet will be shown on my plan as a 30 in. plus $\frac{1}{4}$ in. L-upper or L-lower.

Standard stile width is 1in. and standard gable end thickness is $\frac{5}{8}$ in. This means that on the usual cabinet, the stile extends beyond the gable end by $\frac{3}{8}$ in. The $\frac{1}{4}$ in. increase in stile width makes the stile extend a total of $\frac{5}{8}$ in. past the gable end.

Apply a sheet of $\frac{1}{4}$in. wood veneer-covered plywood, matching the cabinet wood, to the gable end with contact cement. This veneer plywood is sized so that it totally covers the gable end from side to side and from top to bottom. After cabinet installation, install wood door-stop molding around the perimeter of the cabinet end. Door-stop molding is available in most woods. I've used oak, pine, cherry and maple molding.

This molding is rounded on one side and flat on the other. I install it around the perimeter of the gable end, with the rounded side to the inside.

Tip: USE AIR NAILER
Invest in a small air brad nailer and compressor. This nailer speeds up the installation of molding, end and under-cabinet panels, as well as drawer-box trim. If you've ever tried to hammer in brad nails while you're upside down under an upper cabinet, you'll soon realize the value of an air brad nailer.

The molding is slightly flexible so the flat side can contour with any small wall irregularities.

The combined thickness of the veneer plywood and the door stop molding is approximately $\frac{1}{2}$ in., so it's slightly inset on the extended cabinet stile. This type of end-run cabinet finishing looks good and is received well by clients.

The screw holes that secure the end-run cabinet stile to the cabinet rails must be filled with wood plugs so that they won't be visible. I use a $\frac{1}{8}$ in. countersink drill bit assembly with a $\frac{3}{8}$ in. counterbore hole for these screws. I fill the holes with $\frac{3}{8}$ in. wood plugs sanded flush to finish the visible stile sides on these end-run cabinets.

Figure 13-6
Finishing the underside of upper cabinets.

FINISHING UNDER THE UPPER CABINETS

Many cabinetmakers leave the underside of upper cabinets unfinished. This area, while not usually visible to someone standing in front of the cabinets, may be seen by someone sitting in the kitchen. It may not be considered a major issue, but I believe that finishing this area adds a final measure of quality to my cabinet work.

Install $\frac{1}{4}$ in. veneer plywood, of the same type as the cabinets, cut to fit, on the underside of the upper cabinets. The front edge of the veneer will not be visible because the face frame extends $\frac{3}{4}$ in. below the cabinet carcass. If there is an open end-run cabinet, the end edge of the veneer plywood can be hidden by the door-stop molding that you've used to finish the gable end.

OVER-THE-STOVE CABINETS

Over-the-stove cabinets are not as large as standard upper cabinets, because a range hood is usually mounted under the cabinet. Greater clearance is also required so that the client can work properly at the stove.

Figure 13-7
An installed stove cabinet with range hood.

I usually install a 31 in. wide (30 in. standard cabinet with $1\frac{1}{2}$ in. stiles on each side instead of the standard 1in. stiles), $19\frac{1}{4}$ in. high cabinet with 18in. high doors. These measurements are for cabinets over standard size stoves. I use a 31 in. wide cabinet, as I want the space between the base units on each side of the stove to be 31 in. I can then overhang my countertop by $\frac{3}{8}$ in. on each base cabinet beside the stove, which allows for a maximum opening, between the countertops, of $30\frac{1}{4}$ in. for the stove. Widening the over-the-stove cabinet width permits countertop overhang and lines up each upper cabinet with its corresponding base cabinet on either side of the stove.

You can custom-design any size over-the-stove cabinet you need, following the design rules. Refer back to the industry-standard door sizes when designing custom cabinets. The basic rules are: The inside width of the face frame equals the inside width of the cabinet carcass, with the face frame being $\frac{3}{4}$ in. greater than the cabinet carcass in total height, and the door(s) being $1\frac{1}{4}$ in. less than the face frame height. These rules determine your cabinet dimensions.

The stove cabinet that I usually use follows the rules. The face frame is $19\frac{1}{4}$ in. high, with standard $14\frac{1}{2}$ in. wide by 18 in. high doors; the inside carcass width is 28 in., and the gable ends are $18\frac{1}{2}$ in. high. The 28 in. inside cabinet width, plus the total width of the two $1\frac{1}{2}$ in. stiles, equals a cabinet that is 31 in. wide.

OVER-THE-REFRIGERATOR CABINETS

There are two sizes of cabinets that I use as over-the-refrigerator cabinets. I offer the clients a choice based on their requirements.

Most refrigerators on the market today are 32 in. wide, so my normal cabinet width for either style is 33 in. Refrigerators are approximately 65 in. high, leaving a clearance of about 20 in. for a cabinet above this appliance. I use a standard maximum cabinet height of 85 in. made up of a 36 in. base unit and counter top height, plus a distance of 18 in. from the counter top surface to the bottom of the upper cabinet, and a 31 in. upper cabinet height. I want the top of the refrigerator cabinet even with the uppers at that 85 in. height.

The client's choice depends on the clearance desired between the bottom of the cabinet and the top of the refrigerator. A $17\frac{1}{4}$ in. cabinet with 16 in. high standard doors will leave a $2\frac{3}{4}$ in. space and a $14\frac{1}{4}$ in. cabinet with 13 in. high standard doors will leave a $5\frac{3}{4}$ in. space.

Follow the standard rules for building either of these cabinets, and install an adjustable shelf in both the over-the-stove and over-the-refrigerator cabinets. If these shelves are not required, the client can always remove them.

OVER-THE -SINK CABINET

Extra clearance is required when working at the sink. Therefore, over-the-sink cabinets, when installed, are not usually full-height cabinets. Standard widths are used, a 36 in. wide cabinet in most cases. However, the height is the same as the over-the-stove cabinet at 19¼ in.

The use of this reduced-height sink upper is by no means a hard and fast design rule. I have used both standard full height and reduced-height uppers over the sink. I will usually install under-cabinet lighting on this cabinet because, in kitchens where the sink is not at a window, additional task lighting is a practical feature.

NON-STANDARD CABINET WIDTH

There are circumstances when standard cabinet width is not suitable. Typically, this situation will arise when cabinets are to be installed in a "closed run," such as a run between two walls in a kitchen. The wall-to-wall distance is often not equal to the combined width of a number of standard cabinets.

The stile width of standard cabinets can be changed without changing any other cabinet component dimension. This procedure was covered previously under the End-Run Cabinet heading. The primary consideration is the appearance of the cabinets. If possible, we want to maintain a uniform and balanced look.

A sample situation might be a galley kitchen where the wall-to-wall dimension is 107 in. Three 36 in. cabinets would be too large, because

their combined total width is 108 in., and no other combination of standard cabinet widths will add up to 107 in.

There are two or three solutions to this common problem. The first is to design the cabinet run for that area with one cabinet being a drawer bank. As stated under the Four-Drawer Base Cabinet heading, a drawer bank can be any size because it is not dependent on industry-standard sized doors. The 107 in. dimension could be achieved by using two 36 in. base units and one 35 in. four-drawer bank unit. However, this is not always practical if upper cabinets are to be installed above the base units.

Another option is to increase the stile width of the standard cabinet to achieve the desired total width. A combination of two 36 in. cabinets and one 33 in. cabinet in the center totals 105 in. If the outside stiles (on the 36 in. cabinet sides that are against each wall) are each increased by 1in., we will achieve our 107 in. wall-to-wall dimension. The extended stiles will look balanced because the end of each cabinet run will be equal. This can be done with both the upper and lower cabinets on this wall.

There are other solutions that are possible. However, they depend upon the location. The

Tip: COVER IRREGULARITIES
In closed-run situations, I add an extra 1/8in. to each wall side stile so that I can scribe-fit or contour the stile to match any irregularities in the walls.

closed wall-to-wall run may contain a window, so the cabinet combination depends upon the size of the window opening. Possibly a sink needs to be installed in that run, or the client has other specific needs. Many of your solutions will be influenced by client needs. However, you will find this cabinet design system is flexible enough to meet any of those requirements.

CONSTRUCTING A SINK BASE

Sink bases are standard drawer-over-doors base cabinets, usually a 36 in. base, with a false drawer face or drawer face flip-out arrangement over the doors. The drawer face covers the bottom of the sink when the doors are open. I have built full-door sink bases to keep the cost down for the client, but my preference is for a false drawer-over-door cabinet.

Figure 13-8
A sink base with flip-out tray.

A special consideration with sink bases is the use of particle core board where there is a possibility of water damage. Particle core board and water do not go well together. This cabinet is also often used to store cleaning products. For these reasons, construct a standard 36 in. base cabinet using water-resistant plywood, and paint the interior of the cabinet with a good oil-based paint.

Install six legs on this cabinet, with one at the front and one at the back in the middle of the base, to give it added support. This cabinet usually takes quite a bit of abuse because the supply and drain plumbing pipes must be installed here. It is not uncommon to have someone crawling inside the cabinet to install and connect the service. It is also possible that you may have to relocate a cabinet leg if it is in the path of a plumbing pipe. If the client wants a shelf, you may also have to modify one after you determine the location of the pipes inside the cabinet. I usually wait until the installation is complete to determine where, if possible, I will be able to install the shelf. In a lot of cases, shelf installation is neither possible nor practical because of the plumbing.

UNDER-CABINET LIGHTING

Under-cabinet lighting is popular in many kitchen renovation projects. There are many types and styles of lighting assemblies available, including low voltage incandescent and fluorescent fixtures.

I use a fluorescent lamp assembly with this cabinet system, mainly because of the energy-efficiency of this type of light as well as its low heat properties. A warm, white fluorescent bulb gives even, soft illumination to dim under-counter space.

It is best to ask, during the planning stage, if your client wants under-counter lighting, because power must be run and switches must be mounted where required.

The under-counter lighting system is simply a 1in. by 4 in. board, the same type of wood as the doors, mounted on edge under the upper cabinets, approximately six inches from the wall. Use angle brackets to secure this board under the cabinets. Mount the fluorescent fixture (which is available in two, three and four-foot lengths) to the back of the board. I have also mounted the fixture to the bottom of the cabinet behind the board, but the bare bulb can be seen by anyone sitting in the kitchen. The fixture is best mounted to the board, making it almost invisible.

Figure 13-9
Installing under cabinet lighting.

Figure 13-10
Build a base cabinet pull-out with plastic surround.

PULL-OUTS

Base cabinet pull-outs can be a $^5/_8$ in. laminated PCB box, much like a drawer carcass, with a solid wood face, particularly when a deep pull-out is required for pot and pan storage. Another option that I often use is a piece of $^5/_8$ in. PCB with veneer edges to cover the exposed PCB, in combination with European drawer slides. A rail system, called PVC Drawer Surround, is another excellent choice for base cabinet pull-outs.

There is one extremely important design consideration when constructing and installing pull-outs behind cabinet doors. The European hinge used in this design opens in less space than is required for door overlap. In effect, the door

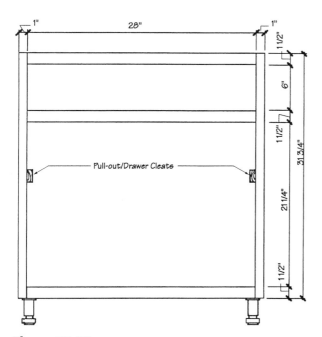

Figure 13-11
Install 1 in. x 2 in. wood cleats on the cabinet sides for mounting pull-out drawer glides. This slightly decreased pull-out width will prevent damage to a door that isn't fully open when the pull-out is used.

mounted with these hinges opens in a space less than $^5/_8$ in. This puts the edge of the door slightly inside the face-frame opening. While this feature is extremely beneficial, particularly when two doors are close together, it means that a pull-out will rub or hit the door. To prevent this, 1 in. by 2 in. cleats are installed on the interior of the carcass, as shown in Figure 13-11, and the drawer glides are mounted to the cleats. The space occupied by these cleats must be taken into consideration when determining the width of the pull-out.

If you cannot afford to reduce the width of the pull-outs by using the cleat method, you can use 170-degree-opening hinges that clear the interior width of the face frame when fully opened. However, the cabinet door(s) must be opened past the 90-degree position in order to clear the space. The need to remind your clients that they must always open the doors fully, as well as the added cost of the 170-degree hinges, may be a consideration. I prefer to use the cleat method with the less-expensive 120-degree hinges in almost all situations.

BUILDING DRAWERS

Drawers are an important and integral component in any kitchen renovation project. The majority of kitchens have a four-drawer bank for cutlery and utensils, plus additional drawers in the base cabinets. Microwave cabinets, with a lower drawer bank, are also an extremely popular addition to the modern kitchen.

In keeping with the design of the cabinets, I wanted to construct drawers that were sturdy, reasonably priced, and easy to maintain. Since

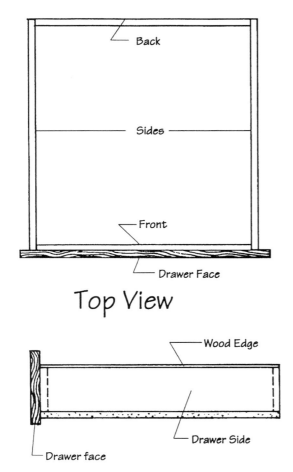

Figure 13-12
Diagram showing drawer assembly details.

strips suitable for the sides, fronts and backs were often left over after cutting the cabinet carcass pieces from 4x8 sheets of material. Also, the plastic surface would be easy to maintain when the drawers needed cleaning.

There are many drawer designs on the market including solid wood, combinations of laminate-coated PCB and metal, as well as all-laminate-PCB material. I decided, based on my research, to construct a drawer carcass in much the same fashion as the cabinet carcass. The drawers are built using industrial grade $\frac{5}{8}$ in. laminate-coated PCB for the sides, back, front and bottom, fastened with 2 in. PCB screws, in combination with high-quality European drawer slides. A wood face is attached to the box as the drawer face and can either be purchased from your cabinet door supplier or made from solid 1 in. by 8 in. material. The solid wood drawer face can be cove or round-over edge-routed to match the style of the cabinet doors.

In five years of using this construction method, I have not had any major problems with drawers. The drawer carcass is heavy, due to the weight of the PCB material, which makes it operate smoothly. The plastic coating allows easy cleaning, so that the client need not line the drawers with protective paper. This drawer style has been received well by my clients, not only because it looks good and is easy to maintain, but also because of the low cost of the unit.

The exposed top edge of the plastic PCB for the drawer box can be covered with plastic iron-on veneer tape or covered with $\frac{5}{8}$ in. wide strips of

the drawer would be opened and closed many thousands of times throughout the life of the kitchen, I wanted a strong, well-constructed drawer carcass. The cost of manufacturing the drawer, as well as the retail price to the client, were also important considerations. Solid-wood drawers would be strong but expensive, so a construction method based on laminate-coated particle core board seemed to be the answer. If constructed properly, the drawer would be very sturdy. The cost would be also reasonable, because

Standard Drawer Detail

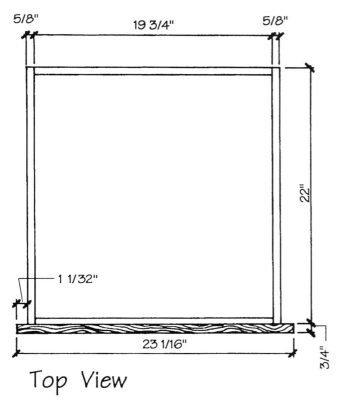

Drawer Detail For 24" Base Cabinet
(Drawer over Doors)

- Opening height space is 6"

- 5/8" particle core board

- 5" combined drawer height

- Use 22" bottom mount european drawer glides.

- Cabinet drawer glide members mounted 1/4" above opening rail

Top View

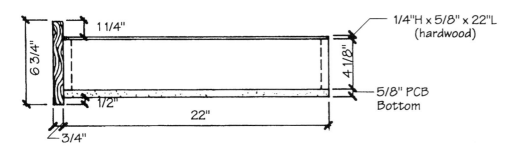

Right Side View

Figure 13-13
Drawer dimensions for a 24 in. wide standard base cabinet.

Tip: USE IRON-ON EDGE TAPE
*Buy heat-activated iron-on plastic edge
tape. It is quick and easy to apply.*

$\frac{1}{4}$ in. thick solid wood strips which are rounded over and finished. The wood edge on the drawers is the same wood as the cabinets and is an attractive accent detail when the drawer is open.

The basic design that I have adopted for drawer construction is based on the same assembly techniques used for standard upper-carcass construction. The drawer is simply a box with two sides, a back, a front and a bottom. The exposed edges of the particle core board are covered with the same wood used for the doors.

I use $\frac{5}{8}$ in. melamine-coated PCB and fasten all joints with 2 in. PCB screws. The bottom board edges are exposed on the sides, so I cover them with melamine veneer tape. The drawer face is solid wood matching the wood finish of the doors. I mount drawers in the cabinets with the European bottom-mount drawer glide. This is an excellent mounting system and is virtually problem-free. Most manufacturers' drawer glides require that the drawer's total width be 1in. less than the drawer opening width. For example, if I am putting a drawer in a 24 in. standard base cabinet with an inside stile-to-stile width of 22 in., the total width of the drawer must be 21 in. The total height of the drawer must also be 1 in. less than the height of the drawer opening. If the opening height of the drawer space is 6 in., the drawer, in total, must be no more than 5 in. high. Drawers for standard bases in this system are 22

in. deep, on 22 in. bottom-mount drawer glides. Given the above specifications, I would need the following pieces to construct the drawer:

1. Two PCB sides @ $\frac{5}{8}$ in. thick x $4\frac{1}{8}$ in. high x 22 in. long
2. One PCB back and 1 PCB front @ $\frac{5}{8}$ in. thick x $4\frac{1}{8}$ in. high x $19\frac{3}{4}$ in. long
3. One PCB bottom @ $\frac{5}{8}$ in. thick by 21 in. wide x 22 in. long
4. Two solid wood strips $\frac{1}{4}$ in. thick x $\frac{5}{8}$ in. wide x 22 in. long
5. Two solid wood strips $\frac{1}{4}$ in. thick x $\frac{5}{8}$ in. wide x $19\frac{3}{4}$ in. long
6. One solid wood drawer face $\frac{3}{4}$ in. thick x 23 $\frac{1}{16}$ in. wide x $6\frac{3}{4}$ in. high

The width of the solid wood drawer face should equal the width of the door or the total width of the doors plus the gap between the doors, when mounted in a drawer-over-door(s) base cabinet. Clearance dimensions are general and depend upon the style of drawer glide used. Refer to the manufacturer's specifications for the brand of drawer glide that you plan to use with your cabinets.

Use two 2 in. PCB screws at each corner joint and 2 in. PCB screws at 4 in. centers on the bottom. The kitchen cabinet hardware supplier in your area should stock small, plastic, colored screw covers to hide the screw heads on the drawer sides. Remember to use countersink pilot holes for the PCB screws but leave them flush with the surface so that the screw-cover caps can be installed.

ADDING A SINK FLIP-OUT

Base cabinets that are to be used as the sink cabinet in a kitchen are considered special units and require some modifications.

Sink cabinets, normally a 36 in. standard base, are not usually fitted with $30\frac{1}{2}$ in. full cabinet height doors. They are built instead as a drawer-over-door cabinet so that the underside of the sink is not visible when the cabinet doors are open. Obviously the "drawer" is not a functional drawer because the sink occupies the space needed for the drawer carcass. The "drawer" is a false face and non-operational. Until recently, this has been lost space.

Now various suppliers sell a flip-out kit that comes with hinges and a plastic tray. You can install this kit on the false drawer front and have a functional flip-out drawer face with a plastic tray inside. It can be used to store scrubbing pads and dish soap. It's a popular option and is an easy item to install. Your local kitchen hardware supply outlet should stock these kits.

ISLANDS AND PENINSULAS

Islands seem to be more popular today as kitchens tend to be larger. They are a useful design feature in almost any kitchen. Island work centers are functional because the homeowner has access to the countertop space from all sides.

Islands are built with standard cabinets, in combination, to create the desired size requirements. Countertops are available from your local countertop supplier or you can build a custom countertop as described in chapter 16. It's best to cut the custom countertop corners at 45-degree angles, and sand the edges smooth and round. One side of the countertop can be extended beyond the island cabinets, so that stools can be used at the island if space permits.

I don't recommend adjustable legs for island cabinet bases because the cabinets are anchored to the floor. Construct a base platform of 2x4 faced with 1 in. by 4 in. hardwood as the finished kick plate, set back so that there is a $3\frac{1}{2}$ in. space back from the cabinet edges on all sides. Anchor the cabinets through the base board to the platform.

Extend the two outside stiles by $\frac{1}{4}$ in. and install $\frac{1}{4}$ in. wood veneer plywood to the sides and the back. Trim the perimeter, on the sides and back, with wood door-stop molding.

Figure 13-14
Kitchen islands are a popular option where space is available.

Figure 13-15
Bathroom cabinets can be constructed using the same techniques.

ADDITIONAL APPLICATIONS

Bathroom renovations can be an additional source of income for the kitchen cabinetmaker. Wood cabinets, in light natural finishes, seem to be the most popular application. Bathrooms, like kitchens, are being given more space during the design process in new construction as well as renovation projects in existing homes. The trend seems to be towards larger, brighter and more functional bathrooms with whirlpools, shower stalls, and all the other new fixtures that are available.

In the past, a homeowner would go out to the local building center and purchase a standard-sized vanity cabinet for a bathroom renovation: One cabinet for the sink, and the project was finished. Today the demand is for cabinets of varying widths, heights and functions. Drawer banks, corner cabinets and pantry-style units are becoming common in the bathroom.

All the standard cutting and assembly principles can be applied when building specialized bathroom cabinets. The only major difference is the

Figure 13-16
A wall-mounted, reduced-depth upper cabinet.

finished cabinet height. There doesn't seem to be a standard height for bathroom cabinets. I've seen cabinets as low as 28 in. and as high as the standard kitchen base cabinet at 36 in. In the last few years, a cabinet height of 34 in. appears to be the most popular.

The client's cabinet height requirement for bathroom cabinets can be easily achieved by simply changing the height of the gable ends and the back. For example, if you require a run of 34 in.-high cabinets, reduce the dimension by 2 in. The base gable ends and back would be 29 in. high instead of the regular 31 in. Otherwise, the base units would follow the standard system.

Upper cabinet size and assembly procedures for the bathroom are identical to the kitchen applications with the exception of cabinet depth. Bathroom upper cabinets are not as deep as the standard kitchen upper cabinets. However, an alteration in depth is easily accomplished by reducing the width of the gable ends, bottom, and top boards. Cabinets over the sink base may be only six inches deep, which means the boards would be ripped at $4\frac{5}{8}$ in. instead of $10\frac{5}{8}$ in. All the other standard assembly procedures would apply.

Cabinet end finishing (which is detailed in this manual), adjustable shelving using the hole jig, and door fittings, are identical to the standard cabinet assembly procedures. The adjustable leg feature of this cabinet system is a real benefit in bathroom applications because there is often water on a bathroom floor. Heating, plumbing, and electrical installation needs, often real problems in confined bathroom spaces, are more effectively met because of the added space under the cabinets provided by the cabinet legs and the removable toe-kick board.

CHAPTER *14*

BUILDING THE FRAMELESS CABINET

The European frameless style cabinet can be built using the dimensions supplied in this manual for face-frame cabinets. Dimensions for the cabinet carcass are identical, with one exception: All depths for the bottoms, tops and gable ends must be increased by $^3/_4$ in. to account for the thickness of the missing face frame.

Door sizes are identical in the face-frame and frameless styles. Verify the dimensions by calculating the frameless cabinet's overall width. Doors should cover each gable end edge by about $^1/_2$ in.

The stated width of a face-frame cabinet will not be identical for the frameless style. For example, a 24 in. face-frame cabinet will be $^3/_4$ in. narrower because of the $^3/_8$ in. face-frame overhang. Therefore, the cabinet should be referred to as a $23^1/_4$ in. cabinet. Two $11^1/_2$ in.-wide doors are used on the face-frame cabinet and on the frameless cabinet. The doors on the frameless cabinet completely cover the carcass edges except for $^1/_8$ in. exposure on each side.

DESIGN CALCULATIONS

European frameless cabinets can be an added line

for your business. They are part of the hybrid face-frame style described in this book. The sizes are easily calculated as long as you keep a few rules in mind.

First, the Euro frameless cabinet is simply the hybrid cabinet carcass with a door. The doors are usually melamine-coated particle board with taped edges or, in the case of high-end Euro kitchens, covered with laminate.

Start by building the basic carcass box. For the uppers, you'll need two gable ends, one bottom, one top and a backboard. The base units are the same, but without a top board.

Use plastic edge tape to cover the front edges of the box, and add the door or doors.

Many North American cabinetmakers have adopted the Euro cabinet as an additional line to offer clients. In doing so, they are using the standard imperial sizes. You'll often see the Euro cabinets in 24 in., 27 in., 30 in., and so on. Because the doors are often made of the same material as the carcass, it's a simple matter to build the cabinet in any size.

One important rule must be remembered: The width of the door or doors is $^1/_4$ in. less than the

Tip: APPLY EDGE TAPE FIRST
Prior to cross-cutting the $^5/_8$ in. PCB to size, apply the edge tape. As you cut the boards, you'll get a nice clean, sharp cut on the edge tape.

cabinet width, and the door height is the same as the carcass height.

Because of this flexibility, the cabinets can be made to any size required. Take a 24 in. standard upper cabinet as an example. Two 31 in. by $11\frac{1}{4}$ in. wide gable ends, two 23 in. by $11\frac{1}{4}$ in. boards for the top and bottom, and one 31 in. x $24\frac{1}{4}$ in. backboard are required when you build the carcass. Two doors, each 12 in. wide by 31 in. high, are cut from the same $\frac{5}{8}$ in. melamine PCB material. Tape all exposed edges, cut two shelves at $11\frac{1}{4}$ in. by $22\frac{7}{8}$ in. wide, and you have a 24 in. Euro style cabinet.

Simple and inexpensive. And you're not limited to any height or width. The cabinet can be any size desired, as long as you follow the assembly procedures as outlined for the hybrid cabinet, and keep the door rule in mind. The number of doors per cabinet depends on its width, but is the same as the width-to-door requirements for the hybrid cabinets.

The Euro cabinet is a good, simple choice for kitchen and bath cabinets when cost is a factor. A 24 in. upper cabinet in the Euro style has a material cost of less than $25.00. The cabinetmaker can sell these cabinets for a retail price of approximately $50.00 per foot and make a good profit.

A Great Low-cost Option

When your client wants a low-cost, basic cabinet, the frameless version is a good choice. It's suitable for work rooms, laundry rooms, general storage areas, and for basic kitchen cabinets. The carcass and doors are all made of laminate-covered particle core board that's available in more than a dozen colors.

If the client likes the European style cabinet, a higher quality version can be made using the same dimensions. Carcass edges and doors can be covered with high-pressure laminate for a more durable finish. Colors, designs and surface textures can be applied by simply selecting any of the hundreds of laminate materials available.

Carcass edges can be covered with plastic tape or laminate, and doors made of vinyl-covered MDF can be installed. The frameless option is also suitable for low-cost storage cabinets made from plywood, then painted. I've used this style many times when constructing workshop cabinets. Simply follow all the construction principles for the face-frame cabinet, and eliminate the wood face frame.

COMMERCIAL CASE WORK

The frameless option is easily applied when you have a commercial cabinet application. Because the final finish is determined by the laminate style, you can offer clients a variety of finishes.

Retail store owners often hire cabinetmakers to build their display cabinets. I have found the frameless style ideal in many such applications. Business people also require desks and display cabinets, custom-built to make a statement, in their reception areas. The frameless style, with laminated surfaces, is very suitable. Stores and businesses can be a lucrative source of revenue for the kitchen cabinetmaker.

CHAPTER 15

KITCHEN CABINET DOOR OPTIONS

The question of making or buying kitchen cabinet doors has been a subject of ongoing debate for quite a long time. For years, before using this design system, I made my own doors. Client desires were numerous and I spent a great deal of time and money investing in wood shapers and bits as well as designing and building the necessary templates. When a large kitchen renovation project can require 30 or more doors, construction costs are a serious consideration and can adversely affect profit. Door styles are numerous and, in the case of solid-core doors, labor for gluing up blanks, shaping and cutting, adds up quickly. Often, the next client wants a totally different door style, which again adds to the costs.

Today there are many specialized door manufacturing companies. During the research for this cabinet system I quickly realized that I could not hope to compete with their pricing structure and offer the variety of styles they have made available. Because they manufacture thousands of doors each month, their prices are much lower and their selection is far greater than anything a small shop could hope to achieve.

Figure 15-1
Assembling a frame and panel wood cabinet door.

A typical solid-core oak door contains about $12.00 to $13.00 worth of material and wholesales to the kitchen cabinet contractor for about $30.00. That means there is only about $18.00 difference to cover the labor cost if you decide to make the door. If your time is worth $30.00 per hour, you couldn't hope to come out ahead, so this kitchen cabinetmaking design system includes the purchase of cabinet doors in the design and cost structure.

Companies that supply doors are numerous, their lines are varied, the cost is attractive and you can offer your clients an unlimited choice of door styles. The door sizes are made to industry standards and the added bonus is that these door companies are very competitive. They want your business, no matter how small your orders.

Building the Traditional Door

A customized door may be required for a project. If you can't get it from a specialist, it is possible to build the door yourself, but there will be added expenses because you must account for the equipment required in order to build traditional-style frame and panel wood doors.

The minimum requirement is a $\frac{1}{2}$ in. collet, three-horsepower router or a shaper. Additionally, clamps are needed for the center panel glue-ups. These boards must be trimmed to size and routered so they fit into a groove on the stiles and rails of the door.

Doors have two stiles and two rails which are routered with a stile and rail bit set. The groove is cut to accept a raised or $\frac{1}{4}$ in. flat panel. There are many door styles, including ones that have a raised arch in the top, or top and bottom, rail. These curved or arched pieces are wider than straight rails, so the arch can be cut into the rail before routering.

Building the Euro Door

A European style cabinet door is simple to build. It's usually flat and covered with high-pressure laminate to a size described in the frameless cabinet chapter. Installing laminate surfaces can be a time-consuming process, but the material costs are low.

Cut the door from plastic-coated particle core board, apply laminate to the edges and front face in that order. Inside surfaces of the European door are not usually covered with laminates as they are not subjected to much abuse.

CHAPTER 16

COUNTERTOPS

CONVENTIONAL COUNTERTOPS

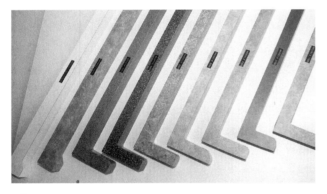

Figure 16-1
There are many styles of post-form countertops available.

Almost every city has a shop specializing in the manufacture and supply of countertops. These are generally the standard roll-top design and are available in almost any size and finish.

The suppliers in my area have roll countertop designs called *Bull Nose, Flat Top, Tradition, Innovation,* etc., and countertop styles such as *Bartop, Regular,* and *Island.* Finish materials are numerous and varied from manufacturers such as *Wilsonart, Formica* and *Arborite.* Costs are reasonable and wholesalers can supply countertops for all your needs.

For best results when ordering either roll-top counters or building the custom tops described in this chapter, use a minimum $25\frac{1}{4}$-in. depth as your standard dimension.

SOLID-SURFACE MATERIAL

An alternative to the roll-top plastic-laminated countertop that has recently been in demand is

Figure 16-2
Solid-surface countertops are expensive but they are becoming more popular in high-end kitchens.

the solid-surface countertop. This is an expensive alternative and installation is best left to specialists trained by the manufacturers. Contact two or three of the local countertop suppliers and speak to them about their pricing schedule, product supply, sample material and literature.

Not everyone can afford the luxury of this countertop, but you may find a call for it in your area. The cost is getting lower as more manufacturers enter the marketplace, so I plan to enroll in one of the supplier's seminars. Once I complete a short training course, the supplier will certify me to install the company's product. If you discover there is a demand in your area, you may find it worthwhile to attend one of these seminars.

Natural Materials

Natural materials such as granite, slate, and marble seem to be more and more popular. The most common is granite and the cost is approximately $100.00 per foot of installed material. The fabrication and installation of countertops made of natural materials such as granite are best left to specialists, for a couple of reasons. First, a cabinetmaker may only install six to eight of these per year. And second, the diamond-tip tools required are costly and a shop owner will need to use them extensively before they pay back on the investment.

Locate a reputable firm in your area, one that specializes in stone work, and speak to them about acting as a subcontractor for your projects. Most are agreeable to that type of association because their sales cost are minimal when you do the proposals. Build in an acceptable profit margin and this line will be an extra source of income for you, with little or no labor cost.

Each stone mason who deals in different materials has varying installation requirements. A few of the granite countertops, for instance, need extra support on the base cabinets as well as additional framing for securing the material, but the last few granite countertop projects I completed were installed directly onto the base cabinets without any special supports.

However, discuss the installation procedures with the stone company to find out what they require. Occasionally, for instance, $3/4$ in. plywood tops were needed on the base cabinets in conjunction with certain materials. Each application is different and it's worth knowing what is needed before you quote a project so that the added cost, if any, can be calculated.

BUILDING A CUSTOM COUNTERTOP

I have seen many custom countertop designs and from them I chose a style that I use in my business. (Refer to Figure 16-3 for construction details.) Basically, the design starts with $3/4$ in. high-density particle core board that is banded with 1 in. by 2 in. hardwood of the same type used on the cabinets. Fasten the hardwood banding to the edge of the particle core board with 2 in. PCB screws and glue. Drill a $1/8$ in. pilot hole with a $3/8$ in. countersink bit assembly at 8 in. centers. Drill the pilot holes as close to the center of the PCB material as possible. Plug the $3/8$ in. holes with wood plugs and sand smooth.

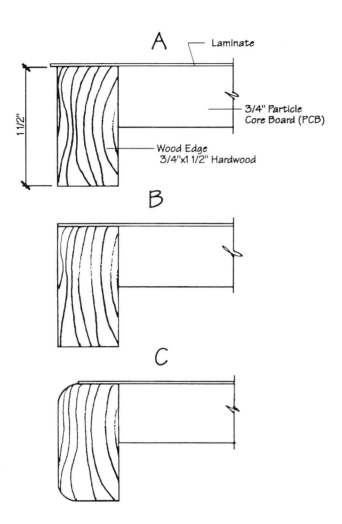

Figure 16-3
Construction details for a custom wood-edged countertop.

Laminate is applied to the surface, trimmed with a flush-trim bit in a router, then rounded over, cutting just to the depth of the laminate. The bottom edge of the wood banding should be rounded over to remove the hard edge and to soften the look of the countertop.

Corners for these wood-edged countertops are angle-cut, fitted with 1 in. by 2 in. wood band-ing, then sanded until they are round, prior to installing the laminate and routering. Backsplash material is usually 1 in. by 3 in. hardwood of the same type as the cabinet wood. Attach the back-splash material to the wall with screws in coun-tersunk holes, and cover the holes with wood buttons.

When designing a kitchen with custom counter-tops, remember that laminate material is usually only available in 4x8 and 5x12 sheets. If possible, avoid countertops that are longer than 12 feet so that you eliminate the need for seams. If you can-not avoid a seam in the countertop, you can buy seam-filler paste from the supplier of the lami-nate material.

Figure 16-4
Wood-edged countertops are a popular alternative to conventional post-formed tops.

CHAPTER 17

▐NSTALLATION

REMOVAL OF EXISTING CABINETS

Unless you're building cabinets for a new home, you'll be faced with tearing out the existing kitchen cabinets and, if they aren't reasonably modern cabinets, you'll most likely find that they were built in place.

Carpenter-built or stick-built in-place cabinets depend heavily on the structural support they receive from existing walls. Therefore, finding fastening devices such as screws and nails can sometimes be quite a challenge. I've seen every fastening device under the sun when I've torn out existing cabinets. It can be funny to see some of the support systems that have been installed.

Be careful to take your time when tearing out old cabinets. Electrical wiring is often hidden, plumbing is sometimes routed through cabinets, and heating ducts may have been directed under the existing base cabinets.

In the interest of safety, I suggest you turn off the water supply and the electrical service to the kitchen area as well as to other rooms nearby. This safety measure will help you to avoid accidents or damage should you inadvertently break a water line or cut a power cable.

Support the upper cabinets with blocks or with a strong wooden box before removing screws or nails. The sudden weight shift downward, when the last fastener is removed, can be surprising.

Always enlist the help of someone to stabilize the cabinet as you remove the fasteners. When dealing with upper cabinets especially, remove all loose assemblies such as shelves so that the cabinet is as light as possible. You'll also avoid the danger of having shelving fall on you should the cabinet suddenly tip. I often remove the cabinet doors as well, to further lighten the load.

Removing base cabinets can be hazardous even though they appear to be sitting on the floor. Rotten floor support systems, or poorly-connected toe-kick platforms may cause the base cabinet to fall forward when the last screw is removed. Again, enlist the aid of another person to support the assembly when removing fastening devices. I've had a cabinet fall because I thought four screws were used to secure the unit, but only two were actually anchored into the wall studs. It can be quite a shock, and potentially dangerous, so be careful.

Tip: USE SUPPORT BOX
Build a support box, slightly lower than the cabinet base, out of 2 in. by 6 in. wood. Use cedar shims to fill the gap between the box and the underside of the cabinet prior to removal. It's an added safety precaution that's often worthwhile.

SITE PREPARATION

Site preparation prior to new cabinet installation is an important part of the process. Verify that water and waste supply lines are in the correct location, and that electrical service is sufficient and correctly positioned.

If you plan to move the sink location, reroute supply lines during the site preparation. The cabinet system detailed in this book incorporates a full backboard on both upper and lower units. Wall sheathing can be removed to allow changes in supply-line positioning, which will be fully covered by the cabinet.

The same is true with electrical service lines. Verify that the outlets are in the correct location and at the correct height. Base cabinet height is 36 in., but you must also account for the added height of the countertop backsplash, which can often add an additional 4 in. to the overall base height. And, if additional electrical service is required, now is an ideal time to have an electrician install new wiring.

Use a long level or straight-edge to check the wall condition. You'll never find a perfect wall, but a wall stud that has badly bowed out, over time, can cause problems during new cabinet installation. If you find a bad bulge in any of the walls, remove the sheeting and correct the problem.

NEW CABINET INSTALLATION

Cabinet installation methods vary, depending on the installer. The primary difference is whether to begin by installing the uppers or the bases. Each method has its merits. There is no single correct way to install cabinets, so find the method with which you are most comfortable.

I will describe my method of cabinet installation based on our sample kitchen layout in Figure 17-1.

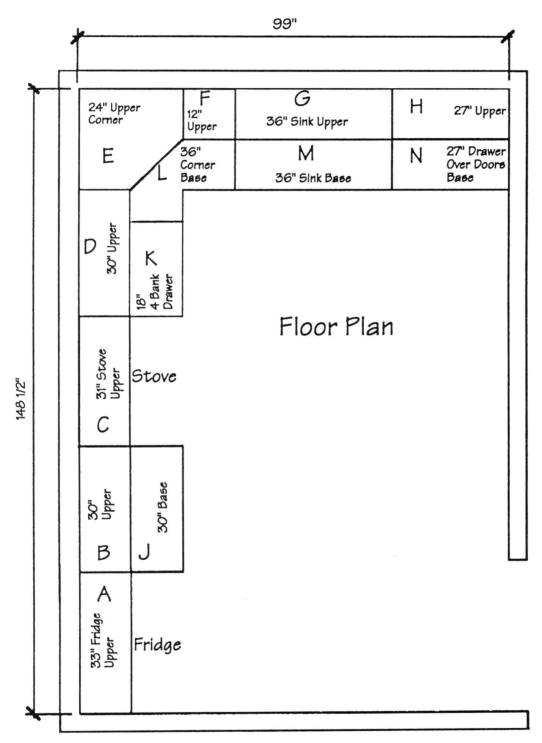

Figure 17-1
Typical kitchen floor plan.

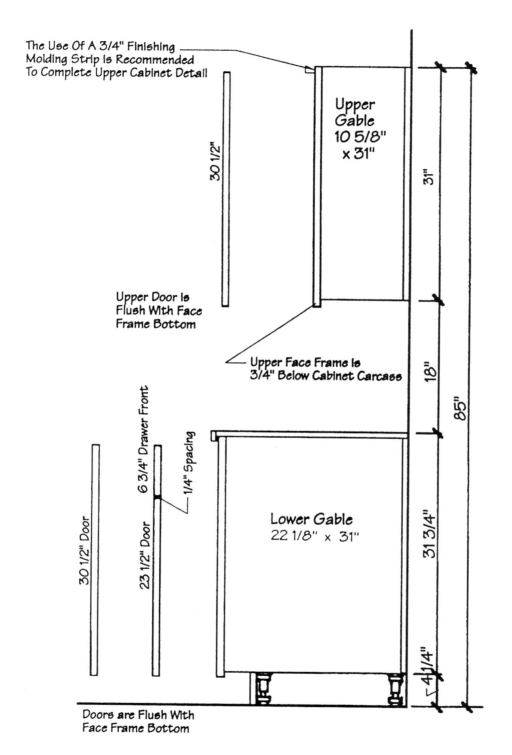

The Use Of A 3/4" Finishing Molding Strip Is Recommended To Complete Upper Cabinet Detail

Upper Gable 10 5/8" x 31"

30 1/2"

31"

Upper Door Is Flush With Face Frame Bottom

Upper Face Frame Is 3/4" Below Cabinet Carcass

18"

85"

6 3/4" Drawer Front

1/4" Spacing

Lower Gable 22 1/8" x 31"

30 1/2" Door

23 1/2" Door

31 3/4"

4 1/4"

Doors are Flush With Face Frame Bottom

Figure 17-2
Standard installation dimensions for upper and lower cabinets.

Figure 17-3
Determine the slope of the floor by drawing a level line where the cabinets are to be installed. This will be your reference point.

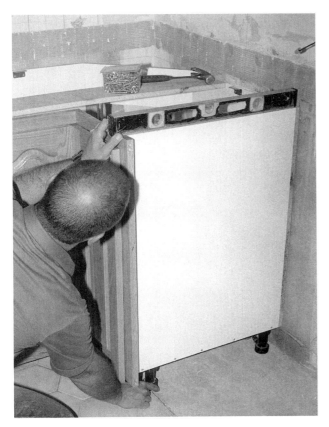

Figure 17-4
Install the first cabinet and level it to the reference line.

1. The first step in cabinet installation is to determine the level or slope of the floor. Draw a level line at a reference height of 35 in. (Figure 17-3) around the room where the base cabinets are to be installed. Measure from the floor to that line at various points to determine the highest point in the room. The highest point will be the smallest distance from that reference line to the floor. All floors have a slope, some more than others, and it's important to determine the high point. If you started installing cabinets in an area other than the high point, you may not have sufficient adjustment range on the cabinet legs.

2. Install a base cabinet at the highest point in the room. Adjust the cabinet legs to their minimum height. Level that base cabinet and anchor it to the wall.

3. Draw a level, cabinet-height reference line around the room. Use the top edge of the installed base cabinet as a reference starting point for that line. Base cabinet N will be used as the first cabinet installed as an example for this installation procedure(Figure 17-4).

4. Place cabinet M beside cabinet N. Adjust the back legs so that the backs of the cabinets are even with the reference line. Adjust the front legs until the cabinets are level, both side to side and back to front. Temporarily remove the doors on the cabinets and clamp the left-side stile of cabinet N to the right-side stile of cabinet M with wooden hand-screw clamps.

5. Drill a $\frac{1}{8}$ in. countersink pilot hole through one stile and partially into the other. Drill a hole,

Figure 17-5
Cabinet stiles are clamped flush, and a 1¹/₂ in. screw is used to hold fronts tightly together.

slightly larger than the screw's body thickness, through the stile, on the screw-head side, to allow the screw to rotate freely in that stile. This will prevent bridging, which is the effect caused when the screw threads into both pieces of wood, preventing the pieces from being drawn tightly together. Fasten the stiles together with three 1¹/₂ in. screws at the top, middle and bottom (Figure 17-5).

6. Anchor the cabinet to the wall with two 3 in. screws through the backboard and into the wall studs (Figure 17-6).

7. Install the remainder of the base cabinets in the same manner. With this sample layout, set the stile-to-stile spacing between cabinets K and J at 31 in., equal to the maximum width of cabinet C. This will provide clearance for a ³/₈ in. countertop overhang on cabinets K and J, and leave a 30¹/₄ in. space for the stove.

8. Install the countertop, scribing and removing material if necessary, so that the countertop fits tightly against the wall. Overhang the small countertop on base cabinet J by ³/₈ in. on each side. Use ⁵/₈ in. screws in the brackets to secure the countertop in place.

9. With the aid of an 18 in. high spacer (I make a spacer box out of 2 in. by 6 in. boards) on the countertop, mount upper cabinet H to the wall with four 3 in. wood screws through the backboard into the wall studs. The cabinet must be level and plumb, with the righthand stile scribed to provide a tight fit to the wall (Figure 17-7).

Figure 17-6
Cabinets are secured to the wall studs with 3 in. wood screws through the backboard.

Figure 17-7
Use a spacer box to hold upper cabinets in place until they are secured to the wall.

Figure 17-8
Install veneer plywood on the underside of the upper cabinets.

10. Install the remainder of the upper cabinets with the spacer box as an aid. Level the cabinets, screw the adjoining stiles to each other, and anchor the cabinets to the wall. The bottoms of the stiles must be even on all the cabinets. Reduced-height cabinets (cabinets G, C and A) should be at the same height at the top of the stiles.

11. Install veneer plywood on the underside of all upper cabinets with either contact cement or brad nails (Figure 17-8).

Figure 17-9
Install upper trim molding on the cabinets.

Figure 17-10
Install the toe-kick board clips.

Figure 17-11
Verify that all cabinets are level and plumb.

12. Cut to size and install trim molding on the top edge of the upper cabinets (Figure 17-9).

13. Cut the toe-kick boards to length, install the plinth clips and secure the boards to the cabinet legs. Use butt joints where the toe-kick boards intersect at right angles (Figure 17-10).

14. Install the cabinet doors, adjust for plumb, level, and for equal spacing between doors on double-door cabinets.

15. Install the drawers and check the operation. Drawers can sometimes go out of alignment if the base cabinet is twisted during installation. Adjust if necessary.

16. Install the cabinet shelves and verify the alignment. The shelves should rest on all four shelf pins. Shelf pins can be thrown out of alignment if the cabinet is racked or twisted during installation. If severely twisted, the cabinet may have to be loosened from the wall and aligned. This twisting can be avoided by making sure the cabinet is level and plumb when it is installed (Figure 17-11).

Try to avoid racking (twisting) the cabinet during installation. Most walls are not straight. Many have irregular surfaces and are not plumb. When anchoring cabinets to the wall, verify that the cabinet back is touching the wall. If there is a gap, use a shim to fill the space. Always check the level, front to back and side to side, as well as the plumb of the cabinet both before and after you anchor it securely.

Racked cabinets will seriously affect the operation of drawers and the proper position of shelves on the shelf pins. It may also cause doors to be off level, affecting both operation and appearance.

All stiles on adjoining cabinets should be flush on the bottom. If there is an error because stiles were not cut the same length during construction, leave the error on top of the cabinet. The top of the stiles on the base cabinets are hidden by the countertop overhang and by the applied trim on the upper cabinets.

CHAPTER 18

CABINET FINISHING

There are many cabinet finishes on the market. They include paints in almost any color, washed stains, and polyurethane. Most finishing products are easy to apply and most will produce excellent results.

In the last three years, most of my kitchen cabinet renovations have been finished with a clear satin polyurethane. Most clients today want naturally-finished wood cabinets, and most prefer oak. I have also finished a few kitchen projects using semi-transparent washed stains, which were easy to apply and produced excellent results.

Large cabinet shops often use lacquer finishes on their cabinet work. They apply the lacquer in spray booths with a paint compressor. This produces a high-quality finish that dries quickly, allowing a two- or three-coat application over a short time period. The spray booth method requires a large space with special ventilation and is beyond the means and space limitations of most small cabinet shops. There are shops that specialize in finishing, and you may want to use their services if they are readily available.

Wood finishing is an art that takes practice and experience. I have tried many finishes and methods over the years. I have taken finishing courses and have read many excellent books on the subject. However, I realize that there is still much left to learn in this field.

My preference over the last three years has been to use an oil-based polyurethane with a good quality brush. I apply three coats, the first coat thinned by 10%, and I sand between each coat. The clear satin polyurethane is relatively easy to use and produces a hard finish that doesn't readily show grease or fingerprints.

Over the last two or three years there has been a move towards the safer, more environmentally-friendly water-based finishes. Latex polyurethane is one of these newer finishes that is water-based, dries quickly and gives off little odor, but I find that the water-based finishes raise the grain, as water will do on wood, and produce a slightly cloudy finish. However, I have spoken with other cabinetmakers who use only water-based finishes, which shows me that the use of different finishing techniques and materials is a personal choice.

Finishing is critical to the final product, particularly with wood cabinets. I would suggest that you start with oil-based polyurethane and then learn as much as possible about the other products on the market. Document the finish used in each client project file, because you may have to duplicate the results when building additional cabinets.

HVLP SPRAY SYSTEMS

High-volume low-pressure spray systems have become popular in the small to medium sized cabinet shop. They are reasonably priced and produce excellent results.

These systems cost under $1000.00. They come complete with a three-stage turbine compressor, spray gun, and hose.

HVLP systems are designed to spray all types of paint, including latex. They deliver in the range of 100 CFM at low pressure (about 5 pounds per square inch). This eliminates a great deal of the misting and over-spray that's common with high-pressure paint sprayers. Most companies offer a range of spray needles that can be matched to the specific paint material being used.

As with all spray paint systems, proper safety precautions are necessary including the correct mask and room ventilation. However, HVLP is less demanding than other systems because of its low pressure.

The low pressure spray system is ideal for a small cabinet shop. It is inexpensive and, when used with the newer water-based paints, can be installed in a relatively small but well-ventilated area.

CHAPTER 19

Retail price guide

There are many books and articles available on the subject of kitchen cabinetmaking. Most of these publications are excellent and are well worth reading. However, these publications seldom address retail pricing. How does someone with a new kitchen cabinetmaking business know what to charge for the product?

I have been operating a kitchen cabinetmaking business for a number of years. When I first began, I was faced with the problem of setting up a retail price structure that would be both competitive and profitable. I discovered that it was a difficult task. I spent many hours analyzing the material cost, labor rate, overhead and profit, trying to formulate a schedule that would be flexible and easily applied. Calculating costs for every project, and then determining a price quote, would be too time-consuming. Since little information on retail pricing was available, I had to set up a number of sample projects from which to calculate my costs. This also turned out to be a time-consuming process, because I attempted to anticipate every potential situation in an effort to formulate an easily-applied price structure.

Quoting clients on their projects is a big part of this business. You will probably get one job for every five that you quote. It will sometimes seem as if you are in the business of creating price quotes rather than building cabinets. I realized from the beginning that I had to develop a retail price structure that I could apply to almost every kitchen project I would encounter.

Common to all projects was the fact that there would be multiple cabinets, both uppers and lowers, measured by the linear foot. In one project, for example, I might have to build 20 feet of base cabinets and 15 feet of upper cabinets. The variable factors in the run of cabinets would be whether or not the cabinets had expensive solid-core doors or less expensive plywood-core doors, and whether the cabinets would contain drawers, shelves, pull-outs or flip-outs.

I did not want to detail a cost for every individual door style. That would be complicated and time-consuming both for me and for the client. I decided to base my linear footage charge on two door-style groups, solid-core doors or plywood-core doors. I calculated the average costs of these two major door-style groups and formulated a retail price for the cabinets based on the client's choice of one of these groups. I would be able to present the client with two simple options concerning door styles. If they chose a cabinet with solid-core doors, the charge would be one price per foot. There would be a lower price per foot for those who chose plywood-core doors. That simplified a potentially complicated price structure.

The next pricing issue I addressed was a per-unit charge for options. I wanted to set fees for drawers, pull-outs, flip-outs and under-cabinet light-

RETAIL PRICE STRUCTURE

- Upper or Base Cabinet linear footage charge based on plywood core doors @ $100 per foot

- Upper or Base Cabinet linear footage charge based on solid-core doors @ $125 per foot

- Upper Standard 24in. Lazy Susan corner cabinet based on plywood core doors (includes Lazy Susan assembly) @ $175 per foot

- Upper Standard 24in. Lazy Susan corner cabinet based on solid-core doors (includes Lazy Susan assembly) @ $200 per foot

- Corner 36in. Base Cabinet with 32in. pie-cut Lazy Susan assembly based on plywood core doors @ $200 per foot

- Corner 36in. Base Cabinet with 32in. pie-cut Lazy Susan assembly based on solid-core doors @ $250 per foot

- Full Height Pantry or Microwave Cabinet based on plywood core doors @ $250 per foot

- Full Height Pantry or Microwave Cabinet based on solid-core doors @ $300 per foot

- Drawer, Pull-Out, or Flip-Out charge @ $75 per unit

- Countertop charge based on either post formed laminate or custom manufactured unit @ $25 per foot

- Under-cabinet lighting charge, including solid-wood light-guard and fixtures @ $25 per foot

ing. The client could then customize any standard cabinet, and I could calculate the price easily and quickly.

Microwave and pantry cabinets would also require a per-foot retail charge. A quote could then be easily calculated based on the footage of the cabinet plus accessories such as drawers and pull-outs.

By determining a simple unit-price structure, I could quote the client a quick price and be rea-

sonably assured that my profit margin would be acceptable to me. I applied this price structure to sample projects, calculated the costs and analyzed the results. Over the course of two years, I've made some minor adjustments to the price structure because of situations I had not anticipated and I now have a simple, accurate, and relatively fast method of calculating a quote for the majority of my kitchen projects.

The upper or lower cabinet charge of $100 per foot for cabinets with plywood-core doors, and

$125 per foot for cabinets with solid-core doors, is based on standard cabinets with adjustable shelves. Corner, pantry, and microwave cabinets are not calculated at this rate.

Corner cabinets, whether uppers or lowers, are charged at a different rate and are considered to be equipped with Lazy Susan assemblies. If your client insists on shelves in the corner cabinets in place of the Lazy Susan assemblies, a price reduction of $25 per foot would be appropriate. However, I have not had a client request this change.

Pantry and microwave cabinets are calculated with the appropriate per-foot charge and are assumed to have upper and lower doors. If drawers or pull-outs are installed, the per-unit charge of $75 is added to the per-foot charge calculation to arrive at the total price. For example, if a 30in. microwave cabinet with solid-core doors is to be fitted with four lower drawers the total retail price is $1050 (2.5 feet x $300 plus four drawers x $75).

A four-drawer base is considered to be a standard base at the $100 per foot charge for purposes of price calculations. For example, a 24 in. four-drawer base unit would be charged at $500 (2 feet x $100 plus 4 drawers x $75).

Countertops are calculated at $25 per running foot times the total footage. In the case of right-angle countertops, I measure and add the total lengths of both runs to cover the cost of extra charges for corner cuts. A right-angle countertop of ten feet on one wall, plus six feet on the wall at right angles to it, would be charged at $400 (16 feet x $25). It is, in effect, a double charge for the corner. However, corner cut charges and corner assembly time adds to the basic cost of the countertop material.

I do not break down the individual costs on the client's quotation. One total price is given for the project unless the client requests different prices based on plywood-core doors and solid-core doors.

The price structure shown is the basis for calculating quotations in my area. Prior to using it in your area, consider any regional influences that may require you to adjust the structure. Material prices, competition, and the amount of work available are some of the factors that may force a change in prices. Obviously, if you live in a remote area and transportation costs add to the wholesale price of material, your charges would have to be increased to maintain your profit. The lack of renovation projects in an area can also result in some aggressive competition, which may force prices down. You may find you have to meet the competitor's price for a while in order to get the work.

The price to the client includes the removal of existing cabinets and the installation of the new cabinets. However, if major room modifications result in extra preparation prior to installing the new cabinets, you may have to add an extra cost for this work. It usually takes me four to six hours to remove the existing cabinets from a standard kitchen. If site preparation takes longer than six hours, I have to charge more for the time.

These retail prices are based on the quality of cabinetry produced using this system. Usually, your quotes will be higher than those from large building centers that supply ready-made cabinets, but ask your clients to compare the quality. Ready-made lumberyard cabinets can be constructed with $\frac{1}{2}$ in. material for the carcass, which is often stapled; backs are usually $\frac{1}{4}$ in. thick, if there is a back at all; the hardware is often inferior, and the fitting and finishing is not well done. Point these differences out to your clients and have them compare the cabinet work. If the client is interested in quality, you will win the quote because, in the long run, your cabinets are a much better value.

The main competition is normally from the middle-to high-end cabinet companies. Often the pricing is very close and the client's decision is made based on style and service. I don't hesitate to compare the final product of this system with any middle- to high-end cabinet on the market today.

DETERMINING COSTS

I am not an accountant and I don't pretend to understand a lot of the principles associated with accounting. However, I realized early in my business career that some understanding of costs, both fixed and variable, is important to the success of any small business. I do rely heavily on experts in the accounting field when developing price structures and business financing programs.

I discovered, by talking to accountants, that there is a common misconception when determining profitability. Many small business operators believe that profit is calculated simply by deducting material costs from the project invoice. They fail to consider the value of their labor as well as

fixed costs such as rent, heat and power. Operating costs such as fuel, vehicle repairs, and equipment purchase are also not accounted for until business year end. The apparent profit of a project is inflated because it doesn't include a percentage of the fixed, operation, and labor costs. This can result in a big surprise at year-end.

You can determine your profit by applying realistic costs to each project. Tracking your material costs and time for each job is important. You should also include your own labor cost. Sit down with your accountant and determine a per-hour labor rate based on the amount of money you want to make and how many hours you have available. Each situation is different. I use a labor rate of $25 per hour applied against each project. If the design, construction, and installation of a kitchen renovation project took 100 hours to complete, I calculate that the cost of labor for that project was $2,500. That figure is determined by the cost of my operation. Yours may be different.

If material costs for project X were $2,500 with labor at $2,500 and the amount billed to the client was $7,000, my gross profit would be $2,000. From that gross profit value, I would have to subtract a percentage of both my fixed and operating costs to arrive at a net profit amount for that project.

It can be a complicated process. However, it is vitally important to your operation that you have a basic understanding of cost accounting. I'm not entirely happy working in that world, but it is a necessary evil if I am to survive and grow. A basic understanding of the issues and the assistance of an accountant are invaluable. Time spent with an accountant is productive and, in the long run, probably one of the best investments you will make in your business.

Project-by-project Analysis

Keep an accurate ongoing file for every project, listing the associated costs. This allows you to accurately calculate the net profit on a project-by-project basis. And it forces you to look at each job on a time and materials basis.

Certain questions should be asked at the end of each project. Was the project profitable? Could I have managed my time better? Did I make efficient use of materials and of employees' time? And, what can I do to improve the net profit of the next project without sacrificing quality?

This file system also provides a historical record of each project. And, while no two projects are exactly alike, there are similarities that can be applied when quoting. It's a process of continual learning by taking the time to critically analyze each job. There's always a question that should be asked: What did I do right, and what did I do wrong?

Adjusting Variable Cost Factors

When reviewing the project file, look at the variable costs. These include travel time, delivery of materials and finished goods, hours of work, and many more, including subcontracted labor costs. These are variable charges, commonly known as operating costs.

Could the costs be managed more efficiently next time? Was it necessary to pay staff at overtime rates to complete the job, when a simple schedule change may have been more cost-effective? Could the finished cabinets be delivered more cheaply by making two trips with the company truck instead of using a rental or delivery truck? There are many questions applicable to each project. It's a process of cost-analysis. If you haven't got the time to lay it all out on paper, at least read the file over, and think about one or two things that can be improved. You'll find that information useful when managing the next project.

CHAPTER 20

THE COMPUTER TOOL

Do you think the computer is only for nerds? Are you avoiding using one in your business? If you've answered yes to these questions, it may pay you to take another look at computer technology.

Years ago, I didn't see much use for the computer in the workshop. As far as I was concerned, it was no more than a glorified arcade game. But, after a couple of years spent ignoring the potential of this tool, I've come to accept it as a powerful and beneficial assistant in my business.

Referring to the computer and all its associated software programs as a tool is an accurate description. It can save time by helping you create powerful presentations for clients. The computer can also produce all the up-to-the-minute financial statements and reports that are absolutely necessary in today's business world. And, computer drawings for kitchen cabinet projects are light-years beyond the manual drawings we have always had to produce.

There are some things you can do to ease the learning process and make understanding the computer and software programs a little less frustrating. To avoid hours of searching in the dark,

try to read and understand all the manuals that come with computer hardware and software. Second, don't hesitate to use on-screen help programs. And third, speak to advanced users, or attend a few night classes to learn the basics.

Cabinet Drawing Programs

Do you draw project plans on a drafting table? How long does it take? Every project we quote requires some form of drawing. In many cases, it can take as long as three hours to complete the plans on a drafting table. Then, if we're awarded the contract, it's necessary to create cutting lists before beginning construction. In all, it's not hard to spend eight hours preparing a proposal, drawing the plans, and laying out the cutting list. However, all this work can be easily accomplished in one hour with a full-featured kitchen drawing software program.

The kitchen cabinet drawing program I use is called Quisine Insite. It currently costs in the range of $2,500, which I consider extremely inexpensive given the amount of time it has saved. QI is a full-featured software package that produces floor plans, elevations, 3D views and cut lists. I can even factor in my basic retail price structure with this program and get an accurate estimate for the client as soon as the drawing is complete. Other software packages are also available, with prices running as high as $10,000. Most will automatically render floor, elevation, and three-dimensional plans. Cutting lists are generated automatically as the floor plan is drawn and, in some cases, a quotation is produced, based on the specifications entered.

Are the drawing programs difficult to learn? Yes, it takes a few hours and in some cases, more than a few hours, depending on your familiarity with computer-assisted drawing (CAD) programs. However, the time spent will be repaid many times over. And the payback time, in terms of investment recovered, is relatively short.

If you are spending an average of six hours drawing, preparing quotes, and calculating cutting lists with a manual system, your cost is $180, assuming a labor rate for your time at $30 per hour. Cutting the time down to an hour means you've saved about $150 per project. The program will have paid for itself over the next 10 to 15 kitchens. But there's more to it than just recovering the time lost because those five hours that were saved can be put to better use as productive hours in the workshop.

Computer drawing programs also help a cabinetmaker win quotations. Nothing impresses a client more than a neat, well-drawn rendition of the new kitchen both as a floor plan and with elevation views. Think about proposals you've requested from contractors. Often the one that stands out in memory is the detailed package with the beautiful drawings.

Another benefit of a CAD program is its ability to change details on a plan instantly. Have you ever spent hours drawing a floor plan, discovered it needed some changes, and then spent many more hours re-drawing it? Those days are gone when your shop is computer-equipped. Plans can be changed instantly and all other associated areas will be adjusted to the new dimensions.

Stationery Creation

Kitchen cabinetmakers don't usually need to send out hundreds of letters and proposals each month. However, most printing shops offer the best price breaks for letterhead, purchase order forms, quotation and estimate sheets in quantities of 1,000 or more. For most of us, that's too much paper to store.

Word-processing software programs, such as WordPerfect and MSWord, have built-in templates for all the necessary business forms. You can customize your own stationery so that it's always up to date. Just recently, the local post office changed postal codes and municipal address designations in my area. If I hadn't been using a computer for all my stationery, I would have had to place a large printing order. Instead, I took five minutes to make a simple change to my template in the word-processing program and my business address was updated on my letterhead and all my forms.

Designing Flyers and Handouts

We covered flyers and direct mail advertising in an earlier section. Both are effective in generating new business. But an ad has to be simple, direct and also attract attention. That used to mean hiring a graphic designer to create a flyer. It was an expensive and time-consuming proposition.

Computer software programs and low-cost printers make it possible for us to design our own ads quickly. There are hundreds of these programs on the market. Pick one that suits your needs and you can design your own ads quickly and inexpensively.

Most programs have clip-art drawings that you can use free of charge. I often use cartoons of carpenters or trades people on my flyers to draw attention to the message.

When it is completed, I print the flyer on my laser printer and take it to a quick-copy business. In volume, these flyers can cost as little as three cents each. The savings realized on a couple of promotions will probably pay for the software purchase.

Contract Boiler Plate

Contracts offer another effective, time-saver through the use of computer technology:

Analyze your quotations over the past six months. Is there information about the business, about your past work, about your standards, or about the quality of cabinets you produce, that you find yourself repeating in every quotation?

Most of our proposals follow a well-defined script. We do this, we use that, our quality is second to none, etc. Standard business background and quality information that we tell to each client, in every proposal, is called *boiler plate.*

Tired of typing the same information over and over? Design a letter with all the necessary information as your standard proposal form. When the next quotation comes along, simply add details pertinent to that specific project at the end of the form. You'll reduce by half the time you spend preparing proposals.

In my boiler plate, the first section on the business's letterhead template is an overview of general information about my business. This is followed by a list of my regular quality features, the ones that are built into every kitchen. The next section I entitle Custom *Features,* details of this specific proposal. Following that information are the terms and financial arrangements. It's that simple. A new proposal has been completed in no time.

CHAPTER 21

WRITING PROPOSALS

We've studied proposals in other sections of this book. However, I want review this area once more in order to stress the importance of good writing skills. There is nothing more important than handing a potential client a neat, well-written and fully-documented proposal. The price quoted is often not as impressive as the clarity of the proposal.

Many tenders have been won based on the quality of a proposal, even when the price was higher than that submitted by competitors. Clients have told me, again and again, "We gave you the job because your proposal was detailed and complete. It gave us confidence in your firm."

Think about times when you've had quotes from subcontractors. Have you had one written by hand on a sheet of paper? Was it the lowest price? Or did the contractor telephone to say the work will cost a certain amount, with no written follow-up, no paperwork, nothing but a telephone call and a price? I wouldn't hire someone under those circumstances and I'm sure other people agree.

I can't believe how little attention some contractors pay to this critical phase in getting approval for a project. After all the work it took to get the client to consider using their firm, they throw that work away. Clients demand a professional approach to their project because they could be spending as much as $10,000 or more on kitchen renovation. That's a lot of money and they're not about to give it to someone who merely calls them on the phone with a quotation.

I recently won a tender where one of my competitors didn't even visit the client's home to take measurements. The client called my competitor and, based solely on dimensions and requirements given over the telephone, the contractor quoted a price. I could hardly believe that a quote could be given so carelessly until I encountered the same situation a year later. Again, I was astonished by it.

Take care when writing proposals. Use the computer and the boiler plate forms. Add the details pertinent to the new project. Present your potential client with a fully-detailed package. You'll soon see the returns because you'll spend less time quoting and more time working.

Presentation

On the first visit to a client's home, take all the necessary samples and documentation. These include door, countertop, and hardware samples. I usually bring along the high quality European hinge and a low-priced copy of it, to show my customer the differences. And I never forget to take a photo album containing pictures of previous projects, letters of recommendation, press clippings and information about my company.

Get all the information you need about the clients' requirements and about any special features they would like installed in the new kitchen. I pay particular attention to the comments potential clients make as they look through the photo album. It's a good way to find out which features are important to them. Listen closely when they say: "Isn't that a good idea?" or, "Wouldn't that be handy in our new kitchen?" If possible, work those features into the proposed design. If your competitors have neglected to do this, their oversight may help close the deal for you.

Presentation is everything. As the chef said, "If it looks good, the customer believes it will be good." Always present yourself, your company and your work as professionally as possible.

When discussing your company with clients, always speak in positive terms. One question that often arises during a client visit is: "How's business these days?" I always say, "Great, we've been really busy for quite a long time." It's human nature to want to choose a winner, and if your business appears successful, everyone will want to be with you. If you tell a client that things are slow and that you need the work badly, he will probably run in the opposite direction. Customers hearing that you're in a slump will imagine giving you a deposit and then losing their money because you went out of business.

One last item that may be worth considering is the estimated project price. I'm often asked for a ballpark figure during my first visit to the client's home. And, as professionally as possible, I avoid the question by saying that it would only be a guess. I tell people that I want to look at all the design possibilities so that I can save them money without compromising on quality. I often say, "I can think of some great design features that I can work in, without a lot of extra cost, but I want to work on it at the shop."

Any guess you make would create expectations, and then create disappointment if your final price is higher. If your quote came out lower than the estimate, your client might wonder where you cut corners to arrive at a lower cost. It's a no-win situation, so I avoid guessing.

Company Overview

It's good business practice to create a company profile for your clients. It doesn't have to be elaborate but it should highlight your experience, give some background information on the company, and describe projects that you've completed.

Prepare a dozen copies, so that you can update them on a regular basis. When you visit a client, leave a copy of the overview along with your business card. It can help remove any doubts potential clients may have in dealing with the unknown as they learn about you and your company.

CHAPTER 22

REFERENCE SOURCES FOR SMALL BUSINESS

UNITED STATES SOURCES

USA Small Business Administration

The Answer Desk, established in 1983, is a nationwide, toll-free information center that helps callers with questions and problems about starting and running businesses. Service is provided through a computerized telephone message system augmented by staff counselors. It is available 24 hours a day, seven days a week, with counselors available Monday through Friday, 9 a.m. to 5 p.m. Eastern Time.

Customer: General Public
Delivered through: Toll-free telephone number: (800) 8-ASK-SBA

Publications

The SBA produces and maintains a library of management-assistance publications, videos and computer programs. These are available by mail to SBA customers for a nominal fee (to defray reproduction and shipping costs). A complete listing of these products can be found in the Resource Directory for Small Business Management. SBA field offices also offer free publications that describe SBA programs and services.

Customer: General public, small businesses, libraries, universities
Delivered through: SBA, SBA OnLine, SCORE, SBDCs, chambers of commerce, libraries, consumer information centers, etc.

SBA OnLine

SBA OnLine is a computer-based electronic bulletin board providing fast and easy help to the small business community. Operating 23 hours a day, SBA OnLine gets relevant and current information to the public as quickly as possible. Services on-line include SBA publications, access to SBA programs and services, points of contact, calendars of local events, on-line training, access to other federal on-line services, data from other agencies, electronic mail, Internet mail, information exchange by special-interest groups, and down-loadable files.

Customer: General public
Delivered through: Limited access:
(800) 697-4636
Full access: (900) 463-4636
D.C. metro area: (202) 401-9600
SBA Home Page: http://www.sba.gov
SBA gopher: gopher://gopher.sba.gov
File transfer protocol: ftp://ftp.sba.gov
Telnet to SBA Online BBS:
Telnet://sbaonline.sba.gov
U.S. Business Advisor: http://www.business.gov

U.S. Business Advisor

When it is completed, this World Wide Web site will be a one-stop electronic link to all the business information and services the U.S. government provides. With the U.S. Business Advisor, small businesses will no longer have to contact dozens of agencies and departments to access applicable laws and regulations, or figure out on their own how to comply. They will be able to download business forms and conduct a myriad of other business transactions. The U.S. Business Advisor is still under development at this writing and is currently on the World Wide Web in a beta version. You are welcome to participate in this development through a feedback mechanism at the web site.

Customer: General Public
Delivered through: http://www.business.gov

CANADIAN SOURCES

Government of Canada Services and Support for Small Business

Distribution Services
Communications Branch
Industry Canada
205D, West Tower
235 Queen Street
Ottawa ON K1A 0H5
Tel.: (613) 947-7466
Fax: (613) 954-6436

Industry Canada is on the World Wide Web with a publication called Your Guide to Government of Canada Services and Support for Small Business. Their home page can be found on the Internet at http://strategis.ic.gc.ca.

General Information on Small Business Loans Act

The Small Business Loans Act, often referred to as SBLA, is a Canadian federal government program designed to help new and existing small business enterprises obtain term loans directly from authorized lenders towards financing the purchase and improvement of fixed assets. The SBLA provides for the sharing of loan losses, if any, between the lenders and the federal government.

Businesses other than farming, charitable and religious enterprises, which operate for profit in Canada, and have annual gross revenues of less than $5 million, are eligible for SBLA loans.

Loans are available to finance three categories of assets: First: the purchase of land required to operate the business; second: the renovation, improvement, modernization, extension, construction or purchase of premises; and third: the purchase, installation, renovation, improvement or modernization of new or used equipment.

Loans cannot serve to acquire shares or provide working capital. Loans can be used to finance, at the discretion of the lender, up to 90% of asset acquisition and improvement costs. The maximum amount of loans a borrower may have outstanding in aggregate under SBLA may not exceed $250,000.

For each loan, a one-time, up-front loan registration fee of 2% of the amount of the loan must be paid to the federal government. This amount may be added to the loan. The interest rate charged by the lending institution cannot exceed the prime rate + 3% for floating-rate loans and the residential mortgage rate + 3% for fixed-rate loans. The maximum period of time over which a loan may be repaid may not exceed 10 years.

All chartered banks and Alberta Treasury Branches, most credit unions and caisses populaires and many trust, loan and insurance corporations in Canada are authorized to make loans and can provide further information on this program.

Canadian Business Service Centers

The CBSCs are designed to improve business access to a wide range of information on government services, programs and regulations. The Centers are a collaborative effort between federal, provincial and private sector organizations. A CBSC has been established in a major urban center in each province.

There are currently 22 federal business departments participating in this initiative as well as other levels of government and non-government organizations. The combination of participants varies from province to province. Western Economic Diversification (WD), Industry Canada, the Federal Office for Regional Development Quebec (FORD-Q) and the Atlantic Canada Opportunities Agency (ACOA) are designated federal managing partners.

Each CBSC offers a variety of products and services to help clients obtain quick, accurate and comprehensive business information. The CBSCs minimize telephone run around, inadequate or incorrect information, and duplication of government services. This enables clients to make well-informed business decisions in an increasingly global economy.

What types of products and services are available? Each CBSC offers a combination of products and services tailored to meet the needs of its distinctive client base. The following is a list of some of the key products and services that may be made available:

- a toll-free front-line telephone information and referral service
- the Business Information System (BIS): a comprehensive database containing information on the services and programs of participating departments and organizations.
- faxables: condensed versions of the BIS products accessed through the automated FaxBack system
- pathfinders: multiple-page documents that list brief descriptions of services and programs available on a topical basis (e.g. exporting)
- a collection of leading-edge business products which include interactive videos, publications, business directories, how-to manuals, CD-ROM products, and external database access.

WHERE ARE THESE CENTERS LOCATED?

Canada/NWT
Business Service Centre
3rd floor Northern United Place
5004-54th Street
Yellowknife, NT
X1A 2L9
Phone: (403) 873-7958
Toll Free 1-800-661-0599
Fax: (403) 873-0101
Info-Fax: (403) 873-0575
Info-Fax: 1-800-661-0825
E-mail: yel@cbsc.ic.gc.ca

Canada/British Columbia
Business Service Centre
601 West Cordova Street
Vancouver, British Columbia
V6B 1G1
Tel.: (604) 775-5525
Toll Free: 1-800-667-2272
Fax: (604) 775-5520
Fax on Demand: (604) 775-5515

The Business Link (Edmonton)
Suite 100, Boardwalk Building
10237 - 104 Street
Edmonton, Alberta
T5J 1B1
Phone: (403) 422-7722
(Information Telephone)
(403) 422-7788 (Center Switchboard)
Toll Free (800) 272-9675
Fax: (403) 422-0040 (Information Area)
(403) 422-0055 (Front Desk)
FactsLine: (403) 427-7971
FactsLine: 1-800-563-9926
E-mail: bscedm@edmcbsc.ic.gc.ca

Canada-Saskatchewan
Business Service Centre
122 - 3rd Avenue, North
Saskatoon, Saskatchewan
S7K 2H6

Tel.: (306) 956-2323
Toll Free: 1-800-667-4374
Fax: (306) 956-2328
FaxBack: (306) 956-2310
FaxBack: 1-800-667-9433

Canada Business Service Centre
(Manitoba)
P.O. Box 2609
8th Floor - 330 Portage Ave.
Winnipeg, Manitoba
R3C 4B3
Tel.: (204) 984-2272
Toll Free: 1-800-665-2019
Fax: (204) 983-3852
FaxBack: (204) 984-5527
FaxBack: 1-800-665-9386

Canada-Ontario
Business Call Centre
Tel.: (416) 954-4636
Toll Free: 1-800 567-2345
Fax: (416) 954-8597
FaxBack: (416) 954-8555
FaxBack: 1-800-240-4192
E-mail: cobcc@cbsc.ic.gc.ca

Info Enterpreneurs (Quebec)
5 Place Ville Marie
Plaza Level, Suite 12500
Montreal, Quebec
H3B 4Y2
Tel.: (514) 496-4636
Toll Free: 1-800-322-4636
Fax: (514) 496-5934
Info-Fax: (514) 496-4010
Info-Fax: 1-800-322-4010

Canada/New Brunswick
Business Service Centre
570 Queen Street
Fredericton, New Brunswick
E3B 6Z6

Tel.: (506) 444-6140
Toll Free: 1-800-668-1010
Fax: (506) 444-6172
FaxBack: (506) 444-6169

Canada/Prince Edward Island
Business Service Centre
75 Fitzroy Street
P.O. Box 40
Charlottetown, Prince Edward Island
C1A 7K2
Tel.: (902) 368-0771
Toll Free: 1-800-668-1010
Fax: (902) 566-7377
FaxBack: (902) 368-0776
FaxBack: 1-800-401-3201

Canada/Nova Scotia
Business Service Centre
1575 Brunswick Street
Halifax, Nova Scotia
B3J 2G1
Tel.: (902) 426-8604
Toll Free: 1-800-668-1010
Fax: (902) 426-6530
FaxBack: (902) 426-3201
FaxBack: 1-800-401-3201
E-mail: halifax@cbsc.ic.gc.ca

Canada Business Service Centre
(Newfoundland)
90 O'Leary Avenue
P.O. Box 8687
St. John's, Newfoundland
A1B 3T1
Tel.: (709) 772-6022
Toll Free: 1-800-668-1010
Fax: (709) 772-6090
FaxBack: (709) 772-6030

Index

Author: Danny Proulx

Editorial Assistant: Gale Proulx

B&W Photography: Danny Proulx

Color Photography: Michael Bowie, Lux Photographic
95A Beech St., Suite 204
Ottawa, Ont. K1S 3J7 Canada
1-613-563-7199

Site and Workshop Locations Supplied by:
Rideau Cabinets
P.O. Box 331
Russell, Ont. K4R 1E1 Canada
1-613-445-3722

Book production: John Kelsey Editorial Services, Newtown, CT
Design: Glee Barre
Copy editor: Kay L. Davies
General purpose clerk: Dag Nabbit

Printed and bound by McNaughton & Gunn, Saline, MI USA